NARRATIVE

OF

A PRIVATE SOLDIER

In His Majesty's 92d Regiment of Foot.

WRITTEN BY HIMSELF.

DETAILING

MANY CIRCUMSTANCES RELATIVE TO THE IRISH REBELLION IN 1798;
THE EXPEDITION TO HOLLAND IN 1799;
AND THE EXPEDITION TO EGYPT IN 1801; AND GIVING A
PARTICULAR ACCOUNT OF HIS RELIGIOUS
HISTORY AND EXPERIENCE.

WITH A PREFACE

BY THE

Rev. RALPH WARDLAW, D. D.

Second Edition, greatly Enlarged.

1820.

The Naval & Military Press Ltd

Published jointly by

The Naval & Military Press Ltd

PREFACE.

LONG prefaces to Narratives, have seldom, I believe, the honour of being read through. If the Narrative possess interest, a tedious recommendation only detains the reader from his enjoyment; and if it possess none, it aggravates his disappointment.—I shall, therefore, be very brief.

The subject of the following Memoir has been connected with the church under my pastoral care, nearly since its formation, in the year 1803:—and, from this, as well as from a circumstance in his religious history, which the reader will discover towards the close of the narrative, it may perhaps be thought, that my recommendations are in some degree, dictated by feelings of partiality. I hope I shall never be so dead to Christian sensibility, as to feel nothing of the peculiar interest which the circumstance alluded to, is fitted to produce. Yet I may say with truth, that the very consciousness of this interest has made me the more jealous and scrupulous in giving the advice to publish; an advice which I never should have given, unless from a sincere conviction, that the Narrative is fitted both to please and to profit; to gratify curiosity, and, through the blessing of God, to impart instruction and spiritual benefit.

The remarks of a private in the ranks, when he is a man of any shrewdness and observation, on the incidents that come within his notice, in the campaigns in which he is engaged, have in them a particular interest.—Whilst we are pleased with the degree of intelligence which they discover, we at the same time, feel a satisfying confidence, that they contain ‘ a plain unvarnished tale;’ unaffected by any temptation, either ‘ in aught to extenuate,’ or ‘ to set down aught in malice.’

The *religious experience* of the writer, I consider as especially instructive.—It sets before us, I believe, in honest simplicity, the workings of a sensible and thought-

ful mind, and of a conscience, which had never entirely
lost its early impressions :—the convictions, and distresses, and reasonings,—the self-righteous and self-confident
resolutions, and the necessary failures and inconsistencies,
of an awakened but unrenewed state;—the natural re-
luctance of man to part with *self*, to plead guilty, and to
depend on grace ; and yet the entire inefficacy of every
thing but this grace either to impart satisfactory and
steadfast peace to the conscience, or to produce in the
heart, a principle of vigorous, and cheerful, consistent,
and persevering obedience.

Of this grace, although, like every other good thing,
it has been too often perverted and abused by the self-de-
ceiver and the hypocrite, the native tendency is, to
" teach" all who receive it, to " deny ungodliness, and
" worldly desires, and to live soberly, righteously, and
" godly, in this present world,—I feel the delicacy of
saying any thing in praise of one, whose living eye the
commendation is to meet, and who is still, like all others,
the subject of remaining corruption, and in danger of injury from its evil propensities; yet, as it is not *himself* I
commend, but the *grace* that has made him what he is,
and to which he owns himself an entire and humble debt-
or, I feel at liberty to say, that the subject of the following Narrative, since he was led to embrace the doctrine
of the cross, has been enabled,—amidst imperfections
and failures no doubt, of which he himself has been much
more sensible than others have been observant,—to " walk
in newness of life," and to shew, that " the gospel of the
grace of God" has been " the power of God unto salvation," when every thing else had failed, and had led only
to despair.

With the exception of occasional corrections in the
use of words and in the structure of sentences, unavoidable in revising for the press the manuscript of one unac-
customed to composition, the *style* is the writer's own;
the work, throughout, having been printed from his auto-
graph, without transcription :—and I pledge my word to
the reader, that a single additional *sentiment* has not been
introduced.

I commend the little volume to the candour of the

reader, and to the blessing of God ;—not without a pleasing hope, that while it may benefit, in a temporal view,
the family of one, whose wound received in the service
of his country, confined him again, even very recently,
from his daily occupation, for nearly four months ; it
may, at the same time, produce higher and more valuable
effects, in the instruction, admonition, and salvation, of
those who peruse it.

RALPH WARDLAW.

GLASGOW, June 14th, 1819.

ADVERTISEMENT

TO THE

SECOND EDITION.

THE very kind reception which the public have given
to the first edition, has encouraged the Author to improve and enlarge the second.   The additions chiefly
consist of a more detailed and combined account of the
Rebellion in Ireland, and the Expeditions to Holland and
Egypt.   These additions, he hopes, will make the reading of the Narrative more pleasant, particularly to young
persons.   He has divided it into chapters, and inserted
the number of the regiment he served in ; but his name
can be of no consequence to the reader.

CONTENTS.

CHAPTER I.

CHAPTER II.

CHAPTER III.

CHAPTER IV.

CHAPTER V.

CHAPTER VI.

CHAPTER VII.

POSTSCRIPT.

NARRATIVE,

&c.

CHAPTER I.

DEAR PASTOR,

I SHALL now, according to the best of my ability, attempt to gratify the wish you several years since expressed, that I would arrange into one connected narrative, the various particulars I then communicated to you, of my previous life, and the exercises of my mind; its various workings, and conflicts, until the period when I was brought to the knowledge of Jesus, as the only and all-sufficient Saviour.

In drawing up this account of myself, my motive is, to record the loving-kindness of the Lord to me a sinner; and if you deem it proper to be brought before the public in any shape, the only object I would have in view, is the good of my fellow sinners, particularly such as have been, or are, in situations of life, similar to those I have been in, or have experienced similar exercises of mind.

Into the *minutiæ* of my early life, I do not intend to enter; and I would make this general remark in the outset, that my chief object is, to give a history of the workings of my mind, during the past part of my life, rather than the particulars of my life itself; but I shall narrate as much of these particulars as is necessary to account for, and illustrate, the history of my mind. I will also notice, briefly, such other things as may serve to entertain or inform the reader.

I was born in Glasgow, in the year 1779. When I was very young, the belief of the omniscience of God, was frequently strongly impressed upon my mind, and the thought of his all-seeing eye, often checked my conscience and restrained me during early life, from gratifying my own inclinations, to the extent I otherwise would have done. I pretty early learned to read; and as I grew

2

older I became increasingly fond of it, even indeed to excess. I read whatever came in my way; but the Psalms of David in metre, in use by the church of Scotland, and the Bible, being the first books in which I learned to read, and having the benefit of godly instruction and example at home, religious knowledge was that with which I was most acquainted. When I was about eleven years of age, I went to the Sabbath school, belonging to the Outer High Church parish, Glasgow, then taught by Mr. Begg, (now minister of New Monkland parish,) and superintended by the parish minister, the late Rev. Dr. Balfour. The chief exercises of the school were, reading the Scriptures, and repeating the Assembly's Shorter Catechism. Dr. Balfour frequently visited the school, after the afternoon's service was over, and staid sometimes an hour, and sometimes even to the conclusion at six o'clock. When the Catechism was repeated, he interrogated us on the meaning of the questions, and instructed us in their import. He questioned us upon the sermons we had been hearing, and gave us doctrines to prove from scripture, by collecting all the passages, that we thought contained these doctrines. The doctrines were the fundamental articles of the Christian religion; and as we read the passages, he would tell us when they were in point, and when not. I was an adept at repeating the Catechism; but as I had no margin Bible to point out the references, I had to range through the whole scriptures, and exercise my judgment, which of course was sometimes right, and sometimes wrong. When I was shown that I had brought forward a passage that did not apply, it made me think better next time; the passages I found out I remembered where to find again; and those that were brought forward by others, I added to my own stock. This was an exercise that did me more good, than all the other exercises of the school: for, in after life, when I had forgotten the Catechism, and the other things I had committed to memory, I did not forget how to find, in the Bible, those passages I had formerly known; and if I happened to be reading the Bible, and came to any of those passages that had been read in the school, it awakened in my mind the remembrance of what had taken place there. I would then recollect something of the impressions that had been made at the time on my mind, and endeavour to remember what was said by the minister on these occasions; but I shall notice this again, in a future part of the narrative. There were rewards sometimes given to any who repeated chapters, psalms, or hymns. The most remarkable instance of this kind that took place while I was in the school, was a present by a gentleman, of Doddridge's Rise and Progress of Religion in the Soul, and Sermons to Young Persons, to be given as a reward to the boy (it was a school for boys only) who repeated best, from memory, Dr. Watts' Divine Songs for Children. We received copies of the hymns, and a time was fixed for the trial. I was very eager to obtain the prize, and even made it a matter of prayer. I wished to have the book, because I had conceived to myself, that it would teach me how to get to heaven. When the day of trial came, the minister was not present, but we were heard by one of the elders. The greater part of the children were very young, and most of them had learned only a few of the hymns. There were only four that could go any length in them, and only three that could go completely through them ; and their merit was so equal, that it could not be said which was best. I was one of those three; but as it could not be determined who merited the book, it was deferred until next Sabbath evening, when it was expected that the minister would be present. He came, and we repeated the hymns to him with such equal accuracy, that he declared he could not give the prize to one more than another ; and to make us equal, he procured other two copies of Doddridge's Rise and Progress; but, as he could not find copies of his Sermons to Young Persons, he bound in Boston's Fourfold State in their place, and I was put in possession of one of them.

* I have learned since the publication of the first edition, that these books were the gift of Mr. Auchincloss, a gentleman who took a very lively interest in the Sabbath schools. He was constantly employed in visiting them, and in giving rewards of various kinds to those who behaved well, and repeated, from memory, psalms or chapters.

I continued in the school about two years.

In 1796, being about the age of seventeen, I enlisted as a soldier in the 100th regiment of foot, or Gordon Highlanders, commanded by the Marquis of Huntly,* then lying in the island of Corsica. When that island was evacuated by the British, the regiment came to Gibraltar, and I, along with the rest of the recruits, left Scotland and went to Chatham, where we joined other parties of recruits belonging to regiments lying in Gibraltar, for which place we embarked at Gravesend, in Nov. 1796. But the convoy with which we sailed, was forced, by stormy weather, to take shelter in Falmouth for six weeks; after which we proceeded to Lisbon, where we lay ten weeks, because the Spanish fleet was at sea, and our's, inferior in number, was watching it. The battle of Cape St. Vincent, was fought while we lay there, in which the Spanish fleet was defeated, and four sail of the line taken, which were sent into Lisbon. The British fleet soon followed, except a squadron left to watch the Spanish fleet in Cadiz. As soon as the fleet had repaired its damages, it set sail for Cadiz, and we went along with it for protection. We left them when we came off Cadiz, and were escorted by some frigates, through the straits to Gibraltar, where we landed in the beginning of April 1797, and joined the regiment.

The general character of the army, for the profanation of God's holy name, is well known; and the temptations a young man has to encounter, from the very general practice of this vice, are very great. The religious instructions I had received, and the knowledge I had of the Scriptures, deterred me from acquiring a habit of swearing: I frequently reproved my comrades for it; and having done so, pride of heart also operated to prevent me from swearing myself, lest my comrades should, in ridicule, retort my reproofs upon me; and this they did not fail to do, if at any time I was guilty of an oath, or any thing approaching to it.

During the time I had been a recruit, and the time I was in Gibraltar, I neglected the reading of the scrip-

* The number of the regiment was afterwards changed to the 92d, which is the number of it at present.

tures. In the regiment, I met with a variety of characters; amongst others with Deists, who attempted to shake
my belief of the truth of the scriptures. I was greatly
disturbed and perplexed in my mind by their arguments;
but I was not drawn into their opinions. Yet I still neglected my Bible, and continued gradually losing the
knowledge of it I formerly had. There was an argu-
ment, which had a powerful effect upon my conscience,
and with which I met all the pleas and excuses for
swearing;—I argued, that if there was no God, it was an
absurd thing to swear by the name of a being who had
no existence; and if there were a God, he certainly would
punish the dishonour done to him, by the profanation
of his name.

There was a society of Methodists in Gibraltar, chiefly
composed of men belonging to the different regiments
in the garrison. They had a small place, where they had
stated meetings for prayer and exhortation; there were
a few of these Methodists in our regiment. Shortly after
I joined it, the commanding officer gave out an order,
for none of the regiment to attend any of their meetings.
What effect this order had, in deterring any from attending
at the time it was issued, I know not: it had not at least a
permanent effect, for I know that several did attend afterwards, and no notice was taken of it. I went to this
meeting place only once all the time I was in Gibraltar,
and I was nearly a twelve month in the place. This
shows what a careless state of mind I was in; for I may
say it was the only religious exercise I was at, all that
time. There were indeed prayers read to the garrison,
every Sunday morning on the grand parade, when the
weather was dry; but the chaplain was always at such a
distance, that I never heard a word he said. There was
a chapel at the governor's residence, where service was
performed through the day, but I never was in it.

I began to fall into company which led me frequently
to get intoxicated; I did not indeed fall into a habit, nor
acquire an inclination for intoxicating-liquors for their
own sake; but had the same circumstances continued,
I have great reason to fear, that an appetite for them
would have been formed, and that I might have turned

out a habitual drunkard. Gibraltar has, indeed, peculiar temptations to produce a habit of drunkenness. The wine is cheap; the place is warm; and in time of war with Spain, there is very little fresh provisions, and what is fresh, is very indifferent. There is a great deal of hard labour for the soldiers, for part of which they get extra pay: by the evening, many of them are fatigued, and actually need a refreshment beyond their ordinary provisions; but those who need the refreshment, are not content to go and get what they require for themselves; they often take one or two of their comrades with them, and having once sat down in the wine-house, they generally sit until either their money is exhausted, or their time; (for the moment the gun fires for the men to be in their barracks, the wine-houses must be emptied and shut, until after the new guards are marched away to relieve the old ones next morning, that no soldier may have it in his power to get drunk before guard mounting.) Those who are treated one night, treat in their turn those who treated them, when they get pay for work.

Many of the barrack-rooms are uncomfortable on account of their size, containing sixty or more men. This greatly destroys social comfort: for one or two individuals can molest all the rest; so that select retired conversation cannot be enjoyed. Any thing of that kind is always ready to be interrupted by the vicious and ignorant, who do not fail to scoff and gibe at what they do not understand or relish themselves. Among so many men too, there will always be found some who take a malicious pleasure in making their neighbours unhappy. This renders the barrack-room quite uncomfortable during the evening; which, as the greater part are employed at work, or otherwise occupied during the day, is the principal time when they can be together. This, along with other things, induces those who have a little money, to spend the evening in the wine-house with their more select companions. Different sorts of vermin are very plenty in the barracks; and it is a common excuse for drinking, that they cannot get a sound sleep, unless they be half drunk. It was customary at that time to settle the men's accounts once in two months; and, as very little pay was given to the soldiers over their rations during the intervals, the greater part had a considerable sum to receive: and then drinking was so very common, that to prevent a multiplicity of punishments, it was found necessary to have no parade, excepting those for guard, in order that the money might be the sooner done; and the different regiments in the garrison, had to take different days to settle their men's accounts, that the garrison might not be involved in one general state of intoxication at the same time. But I hear that matters are differently managed now; the men are oftener settled with, and get a larger proportion of their pay weekly, which prevents them from having so much money to receive at once. The most comfortable time I had, was when I was upon guard. There are many very retired guard stations; some of them in elevated situations, on the very summit of the rock, 1300 feet above the level of the sea, from which the view is truly grand, and where a fine opportunity is afforded for meditation. I sometimes took my Bible to guard with me, but I never made much use of it.

We left Gibraltar, and embarked for England in the beginning of March, and landed at Portsmouth, 18th May, 1798, and went into Hilsea barracks. During the voyage I read something more in my Bible, but much more still in any other book I could find; sometimes it was a novel, sometimes a history or play: sometimes it was a book of a religious cast; but this was rare: I read any thing I could get, to the neglect of the Bible.

CHAPTER II.

We embarked in the beginning of June for Ireland, on board of the Europa of 60, and the Van Tromp of 54 guns. We had a narrow escape from running ashore amongst the rocks, in a fog, upon the Irish coast: the fog, however, cleared away just in time for us to see our danger. A new scene began to open to us: Ireland

8

was in a state of rebellion; and we were but ill informed
of the nature and extent of it. We were told by a pi-
lot, that we got upon the coast to conduct us into Dublin, that the rebels had taken Wexford. The prospect
of being engaged in a civil war, made me thoughtful,
and agitated me not a little. On the 18th June we anchored in Dublin bay, and landed at the Pigeon-house
in the evening. We were here met by Lord Huntly our
Colonel, who had been made a Brigadier General on
the Irish staff. We remained on the mole near the Pigeon-house, which is about 3 miles from Dublin, until
day-break next morning, and then marched into the city
with drums beating, and colours flying, announcing to
the sleeping inhabitants, at the early hour of three
o'clock, the arrival of fresh troops for the support of the
government.

As we now entered into a scene of civil war, I will
take the liberty of stating a few of the particulars of the
Irish rebellion.

The city of Dublin was under strict police: patrols
of cavalry paraded the streets during the day to prevent
crowds from assembling. Numerous and strong guards
were posted through the city and suburbs, and upon all
the roads leading to the country. These guards were
reinforced at night with additional garrison troops, and
large parties of volunteer yeomanry, both horse and
foot. Many citizens of the first respectability, and not
a few of the nobility, were in the ranks of the yeomanry;
and it was not an uncommon thing for a poor Highlander to have a wealthy citizen, or noble lord, posted along
with him on sentry. All the inhabitants were ordered
to be in their own houses by a set time at night.
Strong patrols then scoured the streets and made prisoners of all they found upon them, and entered every
house where they heard any disturbance. Every house
had a written list of the inmates upon the door, and
was liable to be visited during the night; and if any one
was amissing, the owner might be taken up; or if any
were in the house whose names were not on the door, or
if any one was found in his neighbour's house, he was
taken up and fined before being set at liberty. Every

precaution was used, to prevent plots from being formed, and all means was used to find them out. In such a state of society, opportunity is afforded to private malice and ill-will, to injure the objects of their enmity. When I was upon the Grand Barrack guard, two respectable old citizens were brought in prisoners. They were men who were unfit, and very unlikely to have any active hand in conspiracy against the state. They were confined in the guard-room all that day and night; whether they were liberated next day after I was relieved, or removed to some other place, I know not. While they were in the guard-room, they were exposed to the interrogatories of the ignorant and unthinking, who took every such prisoner to be a rebel. They were protected, however, by the interposition of the more intelligent and humane. I had a little conversation with them, and they told me it was their belief, that it was an apprentice of theirs with whom they had a difference on account of bad behaviour, who had, out of revenge, given false accusation against them; such as, that they were holding correspondence with the rebels in the country, &c. They told me that such cases were frequent. Every person accused was taken up, and kept until the case should be examined; and as this, from the great number daily apprehended, could not be instantly done, individuals often suffered seriously, before they obtained their release.

The conduct of persons, whose political sentiments or behaviour, were in any measure suspicious, was closely watched. And when they were found transgressing any of the police rules, their cases were strictly examined. I saw an instance of this, in the case of a respectable gentleman, who was confined in the same guard-room upon another day. He had been found out of his own house after the appointed time at night. He pled that he was only a short time in a neighbour's house: and that the person in whose house he was, was himself a very loyal man, and a yeoman. He said he had always been a very loyal man himself. He acknowledged, that at a certain public meeting, (which had taken place some time previous to this) where a certain political question had been discussed, he had spoken warmly, *too warmly ;* but that that was the only thing in the course of his life, that could have any tendency to create any suspicion of his loyalty. He remained in the common guard-room during the day, and was removed to another place at night. He was liberated next morning when I saw him, and he told me, that nothing farther than his being out of his own house at night was brought against him; and that he had gotten his liberty on condition of paying ten pounds to the fund for the relief of the widows and children of soldiers who had fallen in the rebellion. He said that he happened to have as much money upon him, and that he paid it cheerfully ; for those that were to get it well deserved it. I mention these cases as certain evils arising out of a state of civil war.

During the time we lay in Dublin, the rebellion was raging in various parts of the country, and much blood was shedding. Dublin itself was kept in a state of tranquillity, by the vigilance of the police and the power of the military. Our stay in it was short. On the 1st of July, the volunteer cavalry were employed in going through the city, pressing all the coaches, gigs, and other vehicles, and collecting them in one of the squares. At six o'clock at night we paraded, and went into them, and set off for Arklow. We travelled all night. We were all accommodated at the outset, but fell into considerable confusion on the way, by some of the coachmen getting drunk, and striving to get past one another ; which caused several of the carriages to break down, and others, by running into ditches, to upset. It was conjectured that some of the coachmen did this wilfully, from aversion to the service they were upon. Numbers had thus to walk in the rain, which was heavy ; and several had their muskets damaged, by the breaking down or upsetting of the carriages. One man had his firelock completely bent ; and when he was asked by the people of the villages through which we passed, what kind of a gun *that was,* he told them, it was one of a new construction, for the purpose of shooting round corners.

As we advanced into the country, we began to see the effects of the rebellion. Burnt houses began to make their appearance in the villages, and their number increased as we proceeded. The coaches carried us to about three miles from Arklow, and then returned to Dublin. We entered Arklow in the evening. The place had been attacked by a large body of rebels a few days before, who had been repulsed with great slaughter. They had some pieces of artillery, with which they had dismounted one of the guns of the military, and damaged some of the houses. They had also burnt that part of the town that lay next the sea side, which was composed of low thatched houses and was inhabited by fishermen. It was a very pitiable sight to see this scene of destruction ; and those of my comrades who went to the ground where the rebels had stood during the action, said it was disgusting. Numbers of dead bodies were still unburied ; some of them lying in ditches, and the swine feeding on them. There was a number of prisoners in the place, who had been taken, whom they were trying by court-martial, and hanging; but I was not an eye-witness to any executions in this place. A part of the regiment was stationed in the church, which was not a large one. This was a new kind of quarters, but every part was occupied, pulpit and all; and the grave stones were the place where we cleaned our arms.

The rebels were still in a body upon one of the hills in the vicinity, and kept the place in alarm ; and we had frequently to stand to our arms during the night. On the fourth of July, we paraded in the street at 12 o'clock at night in great haste. The right wing of the regiment got three days bread served out, when we marched away in a great hurry, without giving the left wing any. I was in the left wing, and had only a few crumbs left of that day's rations. We marched very quickly through bye roads ; and when day began to break, we made a short pause and loaded our muskets,—the first time I had done so in the expectation of fighting. There was a high hill before us, (called White Heaps) whose top was covered with mist, and that side which was next to us was very steep. The rebels were said to be on the top of it. Their number, we afterwards learned, was 5000 ; of whom 1500 had firelocks, the rest pikes.

There were about six troops of cavalry along with us : but our whole number did not amount to 1200, without artillery. We ascended the hill with difficulty, without being perceived by those on the top, the mist concealing us from each other. When we had nearly reached the summit, and had entered into the mist that covered it, our front was challenged by the rebel sentinels, who demanded the counter sign. to which the Lieutenant Colonel replied, " You shall have it in a minute." We moved a little further and formed our line. The fog cleared up a little for a minute, when we found that our left was near the enemy, who were collecting themselves into three bodies. The ground betwixt us and them was a wet bog; and the commander of the cavalry told our commanding officer, that if he advanced, the cavalry would not be able to act in such marshy ground as that before us. The fog again covered us, so that we could not see them, and a gust of wind, with a shower of rain, induced us to stand still. The rebels then gave a loud cheer, and then a second, and they began a third ; but it died away, and was not so full or loud as the others. We expected to be instantly attacked, as this was their signal of attack. They, however, had imagined that we were much stronger than what we were; and being terrified by the suddenness of our appearance, in place of coming forward to attack, they fled in great haste down the opposite side of the hill. We stood in uncertainty for some time, as we could see nothing ; then hearing the fire of two guns, we moved in that direction, and got out of the fog, and descended the hill, on the side opposite to that which we had ascended. We then learned that the rebels had gone down the hill ; and, having fallen in with another division of the army, had come upon them before they could get fully formed, and had come close to the guns, when they were fired upon and repulsed. It had been arranged, that different bodies of troops should have mounted the hill on opposite sides at the same time; but we had been sooner than the others, which disarranged the plan. The rebels continued to fly, the cavalry went forward in pursuit, and we followed with all possible haste. When we reached the foot of the hill, I saw four of the rebels lying dead. We continued to march with great haste, and frequently changed our route. We heard firing at no great distance; but the parties were always gone before we came up. The road was strewed with old clothes, oat meal, oat bread, and dough, thrown away by the rebels in their flight. The dragoons killed a great number of them in the fields. The rebels, in their flight, fell in with some baggage belonging to some of the other divisions; attacked the guard, and killed and wounded several, before the rest of the army could come to their assistance; the rebels were then totally dispersed, and a great many killed and wounded; but our regiment never could arrive in time to take share in any of the actions. Several women were among the dead, who were shot in the ranks of the rebels. We had a most fatiguing march, of upwards of thirty Irish miles. In the evening we arrived at the town of Gorey, as did also two other divisions of the army.

One thing I would particularly notice here, is the *ferocity* of civil war; it has barbarities not now practised in the national wars of Europe. In one spot, where seven had fled to a house, in which they were killed, their bodies had been brought out to the road side, where they lay, shamefully uncovered, and some of them mangled in a manner too indelicate to mention. At another place, I saw a rebel, who had been taken and dragged by the hair of his head, which was long, for some distance along the road, and then shot through the heart. It was said, he was unwilling to inform upon the rest of the rebels. Numerous and shocking barbarities were committed on both sides, sometimes originating in animosity, sometimes in wanton cruelty, and at other times in retaliation.

I was witness to a scene of the latter kind a few days after, in the town of Gorey. A man was brought to the back of the camp, to be hanged upon a tree on the road side, by a party of an English fencible regiment. The man was scarcely suspended, when the officer of the party fired the contents of two pistols into the body, and then drew his sword and ran it into it. I then turned

B

14

from the sight with disgust; but those of my comrades who stayed, told me that the body was lowered down from the tree upon the road; that the soldiers of the party perforated it with their bayonets, cut off the head, cut it in pieces, and threw them about, tossing them in the air, calling out, " Who will have this?" They then dug a hole on the opposite side of the road, and buried the body and the mangled pieces of the head, in the presence of a few of the unhappy man's friends. I was informed that he had been a judge in the rebel army for trying their prisoners: that a brother of the officer of the party had been taken prisoner by the rebels, and had been sentenced by this man to be piked to death: and that this was the reason why he had been so used.

Piking to death was what the rebels practised upon those of the king's troops that fell into their hands, particularly if they remained firm in their allegiance. The common method was for " two to stand behind, and two before, the victim, and thrust their pikes into his body at once, and raise it from the ground, holding it suspended, writhing with pain, while any signs of life appeared. At other times, two men, with pikes, would come before the victim, and begin to stab him in the feet, and then the legs, and thighs, and belly, until they reached the heart. At other times they literally perforated the body all over, with pike wounds." Such barbarities could not fail to produce desire of revenge. But, as our regiment had not been in the country during the out-breaking of the rebellion, we had received no injury to provoke our resentment. And as we had not been employed in the execution of any of the rigorous measures resorted to by the government to prevent the rebellion, no one had any ill will against us. We were called into the service of suppressing this unhappy and calamitous rebellion, after it had begun to decline, and we were rather witnesses of its ruinous and distressing effects, than active hands in suppressing it by force. For it so happened, that although we several times pursued considerable bodies of the rebels through the mountains, and were at times pretty close upon them, yet no one of us fired a musket, with the exception of one or two, who did it without orders, on the morning of the 5th July, on the White Heaps : neither was a musket fired at us ; and the only loss the regiment sustained during this service, occurred one morning, when we were pursuing a body of rebels among the mountains. One of our men having fallen behind through weakness, was met by two or three rebels in women's clothes, carrying pails of milk on their heads, as if returning from milking. They offered him drink ; and, while he was drinking, one of them seized his musket, and after threatening to kill him, they allowed him to proceed to the regiment, with the loss of his musket and ammunition.

The sight of so many houses and villages, and parts of towns, burned and destroyed, and the great number of women and children, who were in a destitute state, because their husbands and fathers were either gone with the rebels or were fled for safety, touched most powerfully the sensibilities of our hearts, and diffused a feeling of generous sympathy through the regiment. It so happened at that time, that we had newly received a more than ordinary balance of arrears of pay, so that every man was in possession of money, less or more; and although we were very fond of milk, because we had been long living upon salt provisions, before our arrival in Ireland, yet there were none, who would accept of a draught of milk for nothing, but would pay its price. And if the people of the house would not take payment, they would give the value of what milk they received, to the children.

As this conduct in soldiers is more rare than even conspicuous courage in the field, the truth of what is here asserted, may be the more ready to be questioned. I shall, therefore, take the liberty of inserting a quotation from Gordon's History of the Irish Rebellion. The author of that work is a clergyman, whose residence appears to have been in the vicinity of Gorey, and who had a personal knowledge of what took place there at that time. That author complains of the losses sustained by the inhabitants, from the rebels and the soldiery : he says, " on the arrival of the Marquis of Huntly, however, with his regiment of Scottish Highlanders, in Gorey, the scene was totally altered. To the immortal honour of this regiment, its behaviour was such, as, if it were universal among soldiers, would render a military government amiable. To the astonishment of the (until then miserably harassed) peasantry, not the smallest trifle, even a drink of butter milk, would any of these Highlanders accept, without the payment of at least the full value."—Gordon's History of the Irish Rebellion, 2d Ed. Lond. p. 240.

When we entered the town of Gorey, it was, in great part, deserted by the inhabitants. Nothing was to be procured for money. After the very fatiguing march we had on the day we entered it, we received one biscuit, and one glass of whisky. On the next day, we marched to a considerable distance, in quest of the rebels, and returned back; we got a draught of milk, and one day's allowance of boiled beef, which had arrived from Arklow; but no bread.—The day was very warm, and I was considerably exhausted. That day passed over, and the next day, until the evening, without any word of any more provisions. The dread of having to pass another night, in our present hungry state, determined other two and myself, to go in quest of some thing that we could eat. We saw some who had purchased some old potatoes at the mill of the place. We made all haste to the mill; but the potatoes were all sold. We felt disappointed; but, observing that the mill was at work, we entered it, to see what was grinding. We found a man attending the mill, who said he was not the miller, but had just set the mill to work to grind some barley. There were but a few handfuls ground; and we resolved, rather than want, that we would wait until some greater quantity was done, when we would endeavour to get it cleaned, so as to be capable of being turned into food. After stopping a few seconds in the mill, I began to look about, when I perceived a number of sacks, that were, less or more, filled with something: I said to my comrades, "Perhaps there may be something in some of these sacks that will serve us: we had better examine them and see." We were indeed loath to touch any thing;

but we were in absolute want of food, and were willing to pay for it. Observing a sack about half full, standing beneath another that was full, and was bent over it, we thought we would see what was in the broken sack first. We instantly removed the full sack, and to our great joy, we found the other was about half full of excellent oatmeal, ready for use. The miller's wife came in, in great agitation, and said, that she durst not sell it, for it belonged to a gentleman in the neighbourhood, who was a Captain of the Yeomen. I replied, that we were in absolute need, and must have it; but that we would pay a fair market price for it, which she could give to the gentleman who owned the meal; that he would likely be able to procure a supply to himself elsewhere; that he perhaps was not in the immediate want of it, but that we were, and did not know any where else to find it; and that she might state this to the owner, and that would remove all blame from her. She assented to the justice of this; and said, that one shilling and sixpence was a fair price for the stone weight. The weights were quickly erected; we weighed a stone, paid the price, and set out to get it cooked, leaving a number more of our comrades, who had come to the mill, to be supplied in the same way as we had been. While passing along the street, looking for an inhabited house, where we might get our meal cooked, we met other three of our comrades, who had gone to the country in quest of provisions, but could get nothing but milk, of which they had their canteens full. We agreed that we would give them a share of our meal, for a share of their milk. We then went into a house, in which was a woman with one child. She said her husband was a blacksmith, and that the rebels had forced him to go with them, to forge their pikes. * We told her that we wanted her to make us some porridge, and that she would get a share of them for her trouble. She instantly cleaned her pot, (which was but a small one), and got it on the fire. We procured some wood

* They impressed into their service all the blacksmiths they could find.

B 3

for fuel; and, the first pot-full being soon made, and poured into a dish to cool, we desired her to make haste and get the second ready, for we were very hungry, and what was in the dish would do little to fill us: we then sat down, all six, to satisfy our hunger. What was in the dish, would have been a very scanty meal for three; yet after we had eagerly swallowed a few spoonfuls, we began to slacken our speed, and (although the milk and porridge were exceedingly good) to swallow them slowly, and with difficulty; and we were all reluctantly compelled to leave off, before our little mess was nearly finished, and the poor woman got the remains, and the second pot-full for her trouble. We told her, that we would call back next day after parade, to get another meal. On returning to our quarters, we found that our provisions had arrived in our absence; but as we could not know that they were to arrive that night, we felt satisfied with what we had done. We did call back at our cook's next day; and, after taking a little more porridge, desired her to make use of the rest of the meal as she needed it, for that we had now got plenty of other provision, and were not likely to require it.

The town and adjacent country were in a most distressing state. Numbers of the cattle were going through the corn fields, and destroying more than they were eating. The milk-cows were lowing most piteously for want of being milked. And as the town had been more than once in the hands of the rebels, the alternate movements of the army and the rebels created always fresh alarm to the peaceable and helpless, who were liable to suffer by every change. The rebels harassed those who did not join with them; and when the rebels had to fly, the soldiers harassed those whom they found at home, on pretence that they were friends or favourers of the rebels: so that it was next to impossible, for even those who were unable to take any part on either side, to escape being involved in the distresses attendant on the quarrel.

The following circumstance will in part show this. Three of our men went from Gorey, to the country, in quest of provisions; (I think it was the same three that gave us milk formerly.) They went to a farm house, into which they entered, but could find no one within. They went through all the apartments, but could discover no one. They saw that the fire was unextinguished; the milk and every thing about the house, showed that the inhabitants could not be far away. When they had waited a good while, in the hope that some of them might make their appearance, a young child came into the house. This convinced them that the mother could not be far off. They spoke kindly to the child, and gave it a penny. It then left them, and in a short time re-appeared with its mother and the rest of the women and children belonging to the house. The soldiers told them that they wanted to buy some milk; to which they replied, that they might take whatever they wanted, and welcome. The soldiers said, they did not want any thing for nothing, but would pay for what they got; but the women insisted, that they should take freely what they wanted, and said, that was not the way they had been used by the soldiers that had visited them before, for they took what they wanted without asking their liberty, and sometimes ill used themselves; adding, " We saw you coming, and we were afraid and went and hid ourselves; but when the child came into our hiding-place, and showed us a penny it had got from you, this encouraged us to make our appearance; and God bless you, take what you want freely." The soldiers got their canteens filled with milk, but the inhabitants had no other provisions that they could spare. They then left them, (after giving the children as many pence as they thought the milk was worth,) highly pleased with their visit.

We stayed in the town of Gorey a fortnight, during which time public confidence was greatly restored. The bulk of the inhabitants had returned, and the grocers' shops began to be replenished. There was no whisky, or drink of any kind, to be had when we entered it; but whisky was distilled and sold, some days previous to our departure, which consumed the soldiers' money much faster than the buying of milk did, although the milk was by far the preferable article, had they been

so wise as to have contented themselves with it. We
left Gorey, and had two days march to Blessington,
12 miles from Dublin. Our route led us through a
part of the country that had suffered severely. Almost
every change of landscape presented to our view the
roofless walls of cabins and of gentlemen's country
seats, many of which were spacious and elegant. The
populous village of Carnew, where we halted for a night,
had been almost totally burnt. The inhabitants had
sheltered themselves within the walls of their cabins the
best way they could; but in wet weather, their condition was pitiful. A great part of the town of Blessington had also been destroyed. We pitched our tents
in the rear of the Marquis of Downshire's fine house,
which had also been burnt. A large body of military
was encamped in the pleasure grounds, and great openings were made in the walls and hedges to admit of
a ready communication between the different parts of
the camp, and every thing was in a ruinous state. We
were here put under the orders of Sir John Moore,
then a major-general, and in a few days he marched
with our regiment, and the Hompesch dragoons, and two
pieces of artillery, and encamped in the glen of Eimal,
among the mountains of Wicklow : where several detached bodies of rebels were still in arms. When we entered the glen, which was a fruitful valley of considerable
extent, the inhabitants kept their houses, because some
of the military, who had been there before us, had
spread a report that we were uncommonly ferocious.
But this impression was of short duration; we were soon
great favourites with them, and our camp became a place
of public resort, particularly upon Sundays. The young
men and women were entertained with whisky, music,
and dancing ; to which exercise they were encouraged
by the attendance and approbation of a neighbouring
Catholic priest, who excited the young women to dance
with the military, even with very profane language. This
drew forth the remarks of the soldiers ; and even the
most openly profane among them condemned their own
sins when committed by a priest.—A circumstance of a
different kind took place here, which was remarked

as uncommon among us. Two of the soldiers quarrel-
led, and had a long vociferous wrangle, consisting chiefly
in p ofane oaths and curses. They were not far from
the Major's tent ; (the Major was a Catholic ;) he was
so disgusted at the horrid profanity of their language,
that he ordered them extra drill, as a punishment, and
complained to Lord Huntly, who gave out an order, pro-
hibiting the practice, and threatening to put the Articles
of War in force, and to fine every man in a shilling for
every oath. This was a temporary check to the very
public commission of it, but it was only of short duration ; for the practice was too general among all ranks,
and the order was soon, as if it had never been.

While we lay in this camp, Sir John Moore marched
twice with us into the interior of the mountains, where
the rebels still kept in small bodies. They made a
show of resistance, but fled when we got near them.
We pursued them slowly, Sir John did not allow any to
fire at them, though it might, at times, have been done.
It appeared to be his intention to intimidate them from
remaining in arms, and, by showing them forbearance,
to induce them to return to their allegiance.' This wise
conduct of the general, along with the conciliatory behaviour of the soldiers, had a happy effect. For, during
the time that we were encamped here, the greater part
of them came in, and delivered up their arms. The
whole would have submitted in the course of a day or
two, if the French had not landed at Killala. It was
said, that the only remaining leaders were in the camp,
and had left it to fetch in their followers the next day ;
but that the report of the French having landed, * reach-
ing them in the evening, revived their hopes of a revolu-
tion : and, our marching suddenly away next morning
to oppose the French, confirmed them in the belief that
they were in great force. In consequence of this, they
remained in arms during the autumn and winter, com-
mitting petty depredations, and skulking among the
mountains. It was lamentable to see the ignorance of

* Reports varied as to the number landed : some reports made
them 15,000, others, as high as 30,000.

the people who had been in arms. They were indeed no judges of political questions. Petty local animosity, and an aversion to Protestants, was all that operated with the great body of them; and beyond these, they could not be made to look by those who saw farther.

Their bigotry to the Romish religion was so strong, that although their oaths, as united Irishmen, bound them to " persevere in endeavouring to form a brotherhood of affection among Irishmen of *every religious* persuasion," they were no sooner up in arms, than they began to show that Protestants would not be tolerated. They put many Protestants to death, in the most cruel manner, some of whom were fighting in their own ranks. And had they succeeded in overturning the government, they would not have spared even those Protestant gentlemen that were their chief leaders, nor yet those of their own communion that were favourers of toleration. Their secular leaders, whether Protestant or Catholic, were soon convinced, that because they did not approve of intolerance, their lives would fall a sacrifice to their own party if it was successful. They preferred surrendering themselves to the clemency of the government, as soon as it was in their power, to staying among the rebels; for, although they had forfeited their lives by their rebellion, they had a greater chance of being spared by the clemency of the government, than of escaping the bigotry of those whom they themselves had stirred up to rise in arms against it. One Garret Byrne, a Roman Catholic gentleman, of landed property, surrendered, after the affair of the White Heaps, and was sent to our camp, and was employed by Sir John Moore, to guide us through the mountains, when we went in pursuit of the rebels.

Disaffection had spread among the Protestants of the north, as well as among the Papists of the south; but, as soon as the Protestants in the north heard that the rebellion had taken a religious turn in the south, they were glad to be quiet, for, they instantly saw that their safety (they being by far the fewer number) lay in the preservation of the government. This freed the government from the resistance of the Protestant rebels of the north; for whom, the superiority of their intelligence, were more to be dreaded than the Catholics of the south. Want of subordination in the rebel armies, also, contributed materially to render the rebellion abortive. Their notions of liberty, for which they ignorantly pretended to be fighting, were of such a nature as to render every attempt to train them to arms utterly vain. They said, we are the sovereign people—we are free—we will not be drilled like those slaves of government, the red coats. To be drilled like a soldier was a degree of subordination which they had never been subject to; and, when they had been persuaded by those who stirred them up to rebellion, that they were slaves, and that they would obtain freedom by rising in arms, they could not see the consistency of this, with submitting to the slavery of being drilled like soldiers. Indeed, their actions showed that the liberty for which *they were fighting*, was a liberty to violate the laws of God and man, and indulge in licentiousness, riot, and dissipation, and the cruelties of superstition.

We had a long fatiguing march to the opposite coast of Ireland. We never came in contact with the French, but we were extremely glad when we heard of their surrender, as we were weary with hard marching. We escorted them as prisoners one day's march; their number was then, of all ranks, somewhat about 800. When they landed, they were 1100, (Gordon's History of the Irish Rebellion, p. 294.) There were several amongst them who had been prisoners in Corsica when our regiment was there, and they recognised some of our men, as having been guards over them there.

They had brought a large quantity of arms, accoutrements, and clothing, from France, to equip the Irish rebels, many of whom had joined them after they had taken the town of Castlebar; but the major part left them, and went away with the arms, accoutrements, and clothing they had received, as soon as the French began to drill them. Muskets had been given to five thousand five hundred in Castlebar, but there were only about fifteen hundred that accompanied the French on their march from that place to Ballinamuck, where the French surrendered, when 500 of them were killed, and the rest dispersed. They were also dangerous as well as useless allies to the French ; for they were not disposed to give quarter to prisoners. I heard of an instance of a rebel who killed a soldier that had been taken prisoner : one of the French cavalry instantly cut the rebel down with his sword. This restraint did not suit the sanguinary temper of the rebels; but the French well knew that if their allies did not give quarter, no quarter would be given to them. The alliance was also very incongruous ; for the*rebels were all bigotted Catholics, and the French enthusiastic infidels, who openly boasted that they had lately driven Mr. Pope out of Italy, and had not expected to find him so suddenly in Ireland. They smiled at the simplicity of the Irish when they heard them declare that they came to take arms for France and the blessed Virgin. The priests were treated with the utmost contempt by the French general, although it was his interest to have acted otherwise. There can be no doubt that, although the French had succeeded in revolutionizing Ireland, their religious difference would have produced a new war between them and the Irish.

We did not return to the Wicklow mountains ; but encamped during the autumn, at Moat, 12 miles from Athlone, which is near the centre of Ireland : and, when winter set in, we went into Athlone for winter quarters. The number of the regiment was changed at this time from the 100th to the 92d.

We lay there from the end of October, 1798, to June, 1799. In this place it pleased God to lead my mind to serious and deep reflection, and to begin a work of sharp conviction, such as I had never before experienced. There was a Catholic Chapel, an English Church, and a Wesleyan Methodist Meeting-house in the town. In the Methodist Meeting-house, there were always public prayers evening and morning, and sermon on the Lord's day, and often twice a-week in the evenings. I attended the Meeting-house pretty closely, and began to read my Bible with more than common attention. I reviewed my past life, and found that I was an exceeding great sinner in the sight of God : and God's goodness as my Creator, and merciful Preserver, appeared to my view in a much stronger light than ever it had done before. I read several religious books, amongst which were Baxter's Call to the Unconverted, and Young's Night Thoughts. The subject of life, death, and immortality, occupied my thoughts very much; the conviction of my ingratitude, in sinning against God, often made me weep in secret, and the fear of falling into the hands of a justly offended God, frequently made me shudder. The words of Scripture, "Repent and turn to the Lord," were strongly impressed upon my mind. I saw there was no salvation without pardon, and no pardon without repentance. I wept for my sins, and earnestly besought God to forgive them. I read the Scriptures, and found, as I imagined, pardon promised to the penitent. I followed, as far as circumstances permitted, in point of form, Baxter's directions. I devoted myself to God, and vowed to forsake sin, and to live a godly life for the future. I made this resolution in sincerity of heart, my understanding being convinced that it was my duty to hate sin, because God hated it; and that if I regarded sin in my heart, God would not hear my prayers, nor pardon my transgressions. I then began to attempt the performance of what I saw was my duty. I began to hunger and thirst after personal holiness; but of the nature of justification, by faith in the imputed righteousness of Christ, I had no conception; and of the nature and design of his sufferings, my ideas were very confused and erroneous. It was a sense of sin that pained my conscience, and I sought for relief in personal reformation, and founded my hope of pardon for the past, and of eternal life, in the success of the reformation. I had now commenced. Being convinced that I was liable to many and strong temptations, and that the conquest of sin would be no easy work, I conceived that it was my wisdom, as well as duty, to have recourse to every thing that could strengthen me against temptation, and assist me in the arduous task of working out what I conceived to be my salvation.

When under this temper of mind, I happened, with a number of other soldiers of the regiment, to be at the

C

meeting-house one evening; and after the ordinary service of praise and prayer was over, the preacher desired the soldiers to remain, intimating that he had something to say to us. He then addressed us, on the propriety of joining in a class meeting, informing us how many soldiers had joined in a class meeting, in a neighbouring town, in his circuit. He said that some of us might scruple, because he was not of the same religious principles as those we had been brought up in. This might be true; but he remarked that we had no opportunity of joining with those, who were of the principles in which we might have been educated, there being none in the place; that, if we chose to form a class meeting, he did not require that we should be of the same principles with him in every thing; but that, if we were concerned for the salvation of our souls, it would be for our benefit, while we were absent from home, to be united together, for the purposes of social worship and instruction.—I thought the proposal candid and reasonable, and put down my name, as one willing to join in a class meeting. I thought it would be a means of helping me in the work of personal reformation. For a short time, I went on pretty well in my own estimation, abstaining from any thing that was open and flagrant; but secret sins overcame me, although I had set myself to resist them with all my might; and this broke my peace of mind. It happened, that there were a number of the regiment, and amongst them some of my own comrades, taken ill with dysentery; and several died of the disorder. This alarmed me much. I began more seriously than ever, to contemplate the uncertainty of life. I read seriously, and with great attention, those portions of Young's Night Thoughts that treat on that subject. I entered fully into the spirit of the poet, and applied to my conscience his reflections. My security of life was completely broken. Every night I lay down to sleep, I was afraid I might never awake, and every morning I arose, I was afraid I might die before night. I would say to myself in the morning, " Some of my fellow creatures, who are living at this moment, will be dead before night; and how can I tell

3

but I may be one of them !" This subject never made so
strong an impression on my mind as at this time. I
never was so much afraid of death, except on occasions
of evident danger. I could no longer place death at a distance. I saw myself in danger of being snatched away
every moment in numberless ways, and put the question
to myself, " Were I to die this moment, what hope have
I of escaping hell and getting to heaven ?" and I concluded, that I had no hope of heaven whatever, but
every reason to fear that hell should be my portion.

I then began to look around me, and compare myself
with the bulk of my comrades. I thought I was not so
bad as they were. I began to reason with myself, that
if God was to send *me* to hell for *my sins*, surely those
that were worse than I was, would also be condemned ;
and, if that was the case, how few would there be that
would escape! I would fondly have indulged the idea,
that surely God would not be so severe, as to condemn
so many, and would fain have cherished the hope, that
because I was not so bad as the major part of those I
knew, I should have a chance to escape. But when I
reviewed my past life in the light of the word of God, I
found nothing but condemnation ; for I perceived that
that word took cognizance of the quality of sin, as well
as the quantity, and condemned both sins secret and
sins open : I began to remember the means that I had
enjoyed above others, of religious instruction and information ; and the declaration of our Lord, " To whom
much is given, of them shall much be required," rang in
my ears. I remembered the impressions made upon my
mind by early religious instructions ; I recollected the
resolutions I had made to forsake sin, and the convictions
which had produced these resolutions ; I thought of
my breaches of these resolutions, and my former for-
getfulness and indifference : and more particularly, my
failing in keeping my last most solemn vow I began
to meditate and consider of God's dealings with me as an
individual : and of the account he would require of *me as
an individual sinner*. I no longer durst compare myself
with other men. I knew not the extent, in number and
heinousness, of any other man's sins. I knew not their

secret sins and evil purposes of heart; and as God would bring all manner of sin into judgment, I durst no longer think in my heart that I was a whit better than the most wicked and profane person I knew; for I knew more evil of myself than I had known, or could know of another. This led me to look more strictly into my own heart, and to examine what was done in it, as I found that the word of God discerned the thoughts of the heart. This led me to investigate the *motives* of my actions, and then I found that I did nothing that was pure. I called to mind the past goodness of God, the many mercies and deliverances he had given me; I reflected on my ungrateful behaviour, and was filled with wonder and astonishment that a God of such awful majesty, should have spared such an ungrateful and vile wretch so long; I was led afresh to consider, " What shall I do to escape the just vengeance of Almighty God?" and my resolution was to repent afresh of my sins, and devote my future life, with greater resolution, to his glory. I durst not delay my repentance to a more convenient time, because the fear of death stared me in the face; and I was convinced, that as death left me, judgment would find me. I trembled at the thought of being called, by death, before the awful tribunal of God. I had nothing to look to on the one hand, but a broken law; and a holy, sin-avenging God on the other. This made me earnestly wish for the pardon of my sins, and I resolved that I would do any thing whatever that would procure it.

I read the Scriptures, but chiefly in the Old Testament, often in Isaiah. To the clearer light of the New Testament, I did not so much attend. Its clear evangelical language did not strike my mind with that force as to fix my attention upon it. From those parts of the Scripture that caught my attention, I formed the following opinions :—that God promised mercy to the penitent returning sinner : this gave me a gleam of hope, which I believe prevented me from sinking into absolute despair ; but I did not understand the nature of evangelical repentance, or the way by which the penitent should come to God, in order to be accepted. The state of my mind at that time was this : I thought that if I sincerely repented of my past sins, and did not commit sin for the future, God would pardon my sins. I also promised myself, that if I truly, and seriously, resolved to serve God for the future period of my life, God would on this account, give me strength to resist every kind of temptation, and to overcome every desire to sin. I promised myself, that, by constant endeavours, and unremitting exertions, I should overcome all obstacles, and finally merit eternal life. I saw that God required of the penitent sinner, future obedience : I was convinced that this was just : I thought that God did not require any thing, but what he had given us power to perform, if we were but willing to do so. I resolved to be willing, and to try my strength to the utmost. I thought that if I did meet with any thing that was too hard for my present strength, God would give me additional strength ; but that the only way to honour God was to use the power that he had already given me. I thought it would be affronting God to ask more, until I had first proved the insufficiency of what I now possessed ; and that it would be insulting to Divine goodness, to be seeking that which was already bestowed upon me. Under this frame of mind, I set about the performance of religious duties. I prayed more frequently and fervently; I read the Scriptures with greater diligence and attention ; I abstained from every thing that was in my opinion sinful. But my past sins were still painful to me, because I was not yet assured that they were or should be pardoned. I was, however, certain that if I continued to commit sin, I should get no pardon, but if I forsook sin, I *might* obtain pardon. The spirit of my prayers was, entreating God to pardon my sins, and promising to lead a holy life in future.

While in this state of mind, I went one evening to the meeting-house. and as I was returning to the barracks, pondering in my mind my guilt, as a sinner, and the goodness and sparing mercy of God, the powers of my mind having been buoyed up by the fervour of the exhortations and prayers I had heard, a sudden emotion started all at once into my mind, that my sins were pardoned by God, that God had promised

C 3

pardon to such as me; and that all that was required was, that I should believe that God had pardoned my sins; that God was faithful to his promise, and it would be to me, even according to my faith. This emotion had a powerful influence upon me. It gave peace to my mind, for I took it to be one of those manifestations of the Spirit, spoken of by those who preached, exhorted, and prayed, at the meeting-house. Under the impressions produced by it, I went on very smoothly, abstaining from sins, to which I had formerly been a slave. I now thought myself happy, and promised to myself, that I would now be able to live such a life, as should be pleasing to God, and should procure and retain his favour.

But I must here add, that this impression that my sins were actually pardoned, was not accompanied with any increase of light to my understanding of the way in which God forgives sin. I was as blind to the nature of the great doctrines of the justifying righteousness and atoning blood of Christ, as I had been before. The views which at this time I entertained of Christ's death, were, that he had died to procure the pardon of such sins as were committed by sinners, while in a state of ignorance and impenitence. I believed that had Christ not died, there would have been no pardon for sin, but that his death had opened the door of mercy to penitent sinners of all descriptions. I thought all the design of God, was to bring men to a sense of their moral duty, and to put them once more in a fair way of discharging their moral obligations to him, as their Creator and Preserver; and that he had promised those who repented, his assistance in all things that were difficult, and his protection from outward danger; and that Christ's death justified God, in granting pardon to penitent sinners, on account of their penitence. I had some faint recollection of what I had read in Boston's Fourfold State, and the instructions I had received in the Sabbath school, and from others, and could discern that there was a difference between them and the instructions I was now hearing, particularly on the doctrine of election, and remaining corruption in believers; but I had no fixed ideas on these topics, only just as much as prevented me from thinking that the Methodists were right, in denying, that the doctrines of election, and of remaining depravity in all believers, were taught in the Bible. I thought they were, but they were not any part of my own fixed belief. I read Wesley on Christian perfection; and, although I did not think he gave a sound view of some Scripture texts, perfection was the thing I was striving to obtain; a perfect obedience to the divine law was what I had set out to accomplish ; and the following lines of one of Mr. Wesley's hymns, were, for a time, very frequent in my mouth, and repeated in secret prayer to God ;

> O grant that nothing in my heart
> May dwell, but thy pure love alone ;

and I resolved that my life should be one scene of devotion and of gratitude to God. I continued to go on pretty smoothly for about six weeks, and I thought I had got the better of sinful inclinations ; but when I fancied I was strong, I soon had reason to be convinced that I was weak, had I only been willing to learn ; for I again fell into some sins, which I had flattered myself I should never more be guilty of; and this broke my peace of mind, and blasted all my hopes. I however found means to heal the sore again, after having undergone considerable pain of mind. I again set out by repenting, and trusting in the mercy of God, and resolving on future obedience; but my conduct was not regular, and secret sins, which lay at times very heavy upon my conscience, would overcome me, although I strove against them with all my might.

I continued to attend the various meetings, public and private, amongst the Methodists, while we lay in Athlone. My attendance among them was certainly of great benefit to me, in leading to a train of experience, that materially contributed to make me acquainted with the deep deceitfulness of my own heart. I was indeed slow to learn ; but what took place with me at that time, afforded matter for reflection afterwards. I think upon it still, and see great reason for humility on account of my blindness, in not seeing while I was there, that I was without strength and without righteousness, without Christ, and without hope. I cannot tell how far the gos-

pel was set before me by the Methodists; but I am
pretty certain, from some expressions that I have still a
faint recollection of, that Christ was set before me in
a much clearer light, than I at that time apprehended
him; I had, all the time I was there, continued in a
course of sinning and repenting, making resolutions and
breaking them; and, although I suffered great pain of
conscience, I succeeded in quieting it by the hope of
better success the next time. When we came to leave
the place, I felt that I should not have the same privilege,
of the means of instruction and social worship, at least
for a while to come; and this gave me less hope of myself, and filled me with a greater degree of fear, that I
should be more liable to be overcome by temptation,
when I should not have the help of the means of grace.

I may here mention, a simple incident that occurred
while I was in Athlone. One night I was placed sen-
tinel over a prisoner, in the room in which he slept. He
was asleep, and I did not disturb him; a book lay near me;
I took it up and passed the two hours with it; it was a
book of sermons on Contentment, written by an old
divine, (if I mistake not, a Mr. Taylor of London,) but
it matters not who the author was. He handled it in a
variety of lights, and applied the principle of contentment to the good works of Christians. I forgot all that
I read but the following expressions; he said, that the
genuine disciple of Christ was one, who was willing to
do every thing for the sake of Christ, and, at the same
time, was content to deny all he had done for Christ's sake.
The author pursued his subject in a spiritual sense, and
I was taken with the book, although I did not understand
it. It was, however, written in such a strain of piety, that
I was struck with it; my memory kept hold of the words,
" do all for Christ, and deny all for Christ;" and I would
at times reflect upon them, as strange and mysterious. I
could never understand them, but I could not help being
struck with them; and when the Lord opened my eyes
several years afterwards, I remembered I had read them,
and wondered how it was I did not understand them sooner: but I was then carnal; and the things of the Spirit
were foolishness to me, for I had not spiritual discernment.

We left Athlone, and marched to Cork, in June 1799, to embark for England, and join the army that was forming to invade Holland. After leaving Athlone, I began to fall off in my attention to serious things. I carried Gray's Sermons in my knapsack, to oblige a comrade who was a Methodist, but who had not room for it in his. I carried it to the place of our embarkation, and returned it to him, without having read any part of it. I had read little or nothing of my Bible either, during the march. I found out the Methodist meeting at Cashil, where we stopt a day, and was at worship twice or thrice.

We lay several weeks encamped at a place called Monkton, near Cork, waiting for vessels to carry us to England. I was twice or thrice at a prayer meeting during that time; but although the prospect of danger was increasing, I was increasingly remiss in attending to religious duties; and this was the case with the most part of those who had been joined with the Methodists. There was only one man in the regiment who was uniformly steady and consistent in these things.

CHAPTER III.

I continued in a very careless and listless state of mind during the passage to England. We landed at Dover, and marched to Barham Downs, where we were encamped. About ten thousand troops were assembled at this place in a few days, and Sir Ralph Abercrombie was appointed to command them. Our regiment was put into a brigade under the command of Sir John Moore. Lord Huntly went upon the expedition as Colonel of the regiment, for he was not yet a General upon the English staff. We marched to Ramsgate, and embarked on board of transports, on the 5th of August, and sailed next day for Holland, under convoy of a fleet of war ships, commanded by Admiral Mitchell. A short time after we sailed, the wind became contrary and stormy, and continued so for about three weeks, which was an uncommon circumstance at this season of the year; so that, although the distance was short, the voyage was tedious. This delay allowed time for reflection, but I did not improve it, for whatever were the passing thoughts of my mind, I was not seriously impressed until a few days before we landed. The wind becoming favourable and moderate, we stood in for the coast of Holland, and anchored on the evening of the 24th, near the entrance to the Helder, and began to prepare to land. The Dutch fleet, of eight sail of the line and three frigates, lay in our sight in the outer road of the Helder, and the fleet of Admiral Duncan, of about an equal number, lay at anchor a few miles from them. The fleet under Admiral Mitchell had an imposing appearance; for it consisted of fifteen sail of the line, and about fifty frigates, sloops of war, cutters, and gun vessels, with about 130 transports. The wind, however, became stormy again on the 25th, and the fleet, under Admiral Mitchell, put to sea; but it moderated during the night, and we returned and anchored nearer the shore than before, on the 26th, and prepared to land next morning. The ships of war hoisted the English and Dutch flags together, because the object of our intended invasion was to expel the French and restore the former government. The troops on board of the ships nearest the shore (of which the ship I was in was one) were ordered to land first. Our danger was now more imminent than ever it had been before; the probability of being suddenly called from time to eternity, was more than ever apparent; and I began again to pray and to meditate. We cooked three day's provisions, to carry with us, and were served out with ammunition on the evening previous to our landing; we did not go to rest that night, but kept on our accoutrements, to be ready to go into the boats when a signal should be made. Such a period is one of great agitation and anxiety. The prospect of landing in the twilight of the morning, on an enemy's coast, ignorant of the nature and extent of the danger, where one cannot tell whether we may reach the shore, or be driven back as soon as we land, or suddenly overpowered before we can get assistance. These, and the like, are serious considerations at a time like this. During the night I was often praying in my mind for mercy, that the Lord would spare me; and I put on fresh resolutions, that if I was spared, I would serve God with fidelity and diligence. All my prayers were for the preservation of life: I durst not resign myself to death, because I was conscious I was not prepared for judgment. All my hopes for eternity, were founded in reformation of character, and that I had yet to begin; for had I been cut off, at that time, I had no hope of heaven.

The province of North Holland is a peninsula, formed by the German ocean on the west, and the Zuyder-sea on the east. The town of Helder stands at the northern extremity, where the Zuyder-sea communicates with the German ocean, between the Helder point and the Texel island, distant about six miles. The city of Amsterdam stands on the south side of the Zuyder-sea, the common passage to which is by the Helder. A range of sand-hills runs along the coast of the German ocean, close to the beach, and the country between them and the Zuyder-sea is nearly a perfect flat. Large dykes, or mounds of earth, run along the shores of the Zuyder-sea to protect the tide from overflowing the country, which is below the level of high water. The sand-hills serve for an embankment on the side of the German ocean. The principal arsenal for equipping and repairing the Dutch fleet is near the town of Helder, the greater part of which rendezvouses there; but they are built at Amsterdam and other places in the interior, and floated down the Zuyder-sea, on account of the shallowness of its water, and are fitted out for sea at Helder.

We embarked in the boats early in the morning, and collected at the stern of a gun vessel that lay nearest the shore, where we waited until day-light began to make the coast visible; I continued at intervals offering up ejaculatory prayers to God, for preservation and deliverance. As soon as the coast was discernible, the gun vessel began to fire her guns upon the shore, and the boats rowed off, giving three loud cheers. The fire of the different vessels of war that lay along the shore was dreadful: but as the shot and shells were all thrown at random, the enemy not being visible, it did little damage ; but it probably prevented the enemy from appearing on the open beach, by which means we got safely landed. The enemy's troops were posted among the sandhills at the different points opposite to our extended anchorage, that were most favourable for landing. These points were chiefly at some distance to the right of the place we landed at, where the beach, not being so favourable, was not so strongly guarded. A part of his force was also to our left, near the Fort at the entrance to the Helder, where they had a camp. We formed on the beach as we landed, and began to advance into the sand-hills. Our regiment was near the left of the line ; there were only a few of the enemy's picquets that appeared in our front, who retired as we advanced: but the troops on the right had not proceeded far before they fell in with a division of the enemy, when a smart action began. The enemy were quickly driven farther to the right, but fresh columns soon arriving, the action became increasingly warm, but our troops continued to press upon the enemy, and took up a position across the sand-hills, to cover the right of the debarkation. Sir John Moore's brigade, in which our regiment was, penetrated also across them as soon as possible, and took up a position to cover the left.

The sand-hills at this place are not of great breadth; the road from Helder to the interior runs along the interior side of them, the peninsula at this place is narrow, and the ground between the sand-hills and the Zuyder-sea is a flat, in many parts swampy. As soon as the first party of our regiment had reached the further side of the sand-hills, they descried that part of the enemy's force that had been posted on our left, passing along the Helder road to join their forces that were engaged with our right. They were composed of horse artillery, cavalry, and infantry. As soon as they observed our advance picquets, they left the road, and made a circuit through the flat ground to their left ; and when they were out of the reach of musketry they made a pause, and fired two field pieces at us, which did us no hurt, and then passed on and joined their own troops. The fire of the ships of war that were anchored to the right and left of the point of debarkation, prevented the enemy from attempting to march along the beach to disturb the landing. They also protected the right flank of the troops that were engaged with the enemy, but he attacked their front with his infantry, and their left flank with his artillery; which he kept upon the flat ground, on the inside of the sand-hills, protected by his cavalry. Indeed infantry were the only troops that were capable of fighting among the sand-hills. Fresh columns continuing to arrive during the course of the day, to the support of the enemy, he maintained the contest and renewed his efforts to dislodge our troops, but as they also were reinforced by those that continued to land, they repulsed all his attacks and gained ground; but, as we had neither artillery nor cavalry, we dared not to attack his that were posted in the plain, nor was it expedient to advance far until the army should all be landed. The enemy continued his efforts from 5 o'clock in the morning till 4 o'clock in the afternoon, when the army was nearly all landed, and some pieces of artillery were brought to bear upon the enemy's cavalry and artillery. The troops then charged his infantry, and drove them beyond Challantes Ogg, a place where an inundation of water from the Zuyder Sea contracts the peninsula nearly to the breadth of the sand-hills. The enemy then retreated into the interior, and left us in possession of our position, which separated him from the Helder. Another fleet of transports, with five thousand additional troops from England, appeared at sea in the afternoon, and anchored in the evening. Our regiment was not engaged through this day; but Sir John Moore's brigade was destined to attack the batteries, and town of Helder, next morning, if the enemy's garrison still remained in them. The loss of the army during this day's conflict was about a thousand men killed and wounded. Our regiment lost sixteen men, who were drowned in the act of landing, the boat having struck on a bank at some distance from the shore; the men got out of the boat, but got into deep water before they reached the beach, and the swell having increased at the time they were landing, they, along with several seamen belonging to the boat, were drowned. I knew most of them; one

D

of them was a particular acquaintance, whose death made a strong impression on my mind.

As soon as it was fully dark, our brigade marched away for the Helder. There is something impressive in a march under the cloud of night, in a strange land where we cannot tell the danger we are in, and have to move forward in solemn silence. It was ordered, that no man was to speak above his breath during the march; and all orders to halt, or move forward, were given the same way. We had frequent stops, which made us, who were not in the front, often wonder what was the matter. Such a march is a service in which the mind undergoes much harassing anxiety, and the body much fatigue. Having come near to the Helder, we halted, and lay under arms, in a state of great anxiety, until day-light, several of their ships of war were then seen at anchor near the town, but they got quickly under weigh, and their whole fleet anchored in the Zuyder sea, about 12 miles from the Helder; which was the farthest distance they could go to on account of the shallowness of the water. After waiting some time we obtained information that the enemy had evacuated the various forts and batteries about the place. We sent out small detachments, who found that it was so, and we then entered the place, and put guards in the different works. When I reflected on the dangers we had escaped, I was filled with wonder; but I soon forgot them all; and during the few days that we lay in the town of Helder, my conduct, in place of being better, was worse than ordinary.

The transports, and a number of our frigates, came into the Helder next day, and the artillery, cavalry, and stores, were landed in the harbour. The day following, the ships of the line came in, and Admiral Mitchel went forward to the Dutch fleet, with a squadron of nine sail of the line, and five frigates. The Dutch fleet then surrendered without firing a shot, and hoisted the orange flag. Their crews were in a state of mutiny at the time, partly out of disaffection to the new republican goverment, but more particularly for want of pay. When they were ordered to prepare for action they refused to fight, and threw the balls and cartridges into the sea. It would indeed, have been a useless waste of blood for them to

have resisted, for if the squadron that went to them had
not been sufficient to have reduced them, there were
more than enough of war ships, of all descriptions, at
hand to have completely overwhelmed them; for after
the batteries of the Helder were in our possession,
they had no way of saving their ships to their country
but by taking out their guns and masts to lighten them,
and towing them through the shallow water to some of
the ports in the interior, out of our reach. And why they
did not do so is not easily accounted for. Besides this
fleet of eight sail of the line, three frigates, and a sloop,
there were two sail of the line, eleven frigates and smaller vessels of war, and three East India ships lying in the
harbour, in various conditions. A large quantity of ammunition and stores, and a great number of cannon for
the equipment of ships, were found in the arsenal, ex.
clusive of the guns and mortars that were on the batteries, many of which were brass.

The army lay among the sand-hills, where it had fought
on the day of landing, until the 1st September, when the
artillery and cavalry being landed, it moved forward into
the interior of the country. Our regiment left the Helder, another occupying it, and joined the army, which
took up a position in the afternoon, upon one of those
huge dykes that are in Holland, which extended from
the German Ocean, where we posted our right, to the
Zuyder Sea where we posted our left, a distance of
about eight miles. We occupied it, at all the parts that
were passable, and threw up works upon it, particularly at
the extremities. It formed a most excellent position of
defence in such a flat country, on account of its thick-
ness and height. The top of it was so broad that any
carriages had full liberty to pass, and was one of the
best roads in the country; and it was not made in a
straight line, but bent in curves, like the bastions of a
garrison line wall. A large ditch runs the whole length
in front of it, with large reservoirs of water in the curves.
The use of this dyke was to prevent the rain that falls in
the winter, on the south side of it, from flooding the
country on the north side, where the level is lower. The
reservoirs in the curves of the dyke receive the

water, and there are sluices that are opened to allow it
to pass by degrees, under the dyke, into a large canal,
a little in the rear of it, from whence it is let out into the
sea, when the tide is low. We had no tents, but were
lodged in the farm houses, which, in Holland, are large,
and of a peculiar construction, having the byre, stable,
hay-loft, and barn, under one large oblong square roof,
made of thatch. A great number of these houses were
ranged at such regular distances, along the banks of the
canals, in the rear of the dyke, that they formed convenient cantonments ; and each house contained from
one to two hundred, who slept in a loft among the hay,
without any other covering than their great coats and
the hay. The fields are all divided by broad and deep
ditches, in place of hedges, which are only to be seen upon parts of the road sides, and round the orchards at
the farm houses and gentlemen's seats. All the ditches
have communications with the large canals that communicate with the sea. A great number of wind mills,
are employed in forcing the water up into the canals,
which are above the level of the ground in the winter
time, and in forcing the water into the ditches whose
elevation is highest, from whence it flows over locks into
the lower ditches in the summer season, so that the
ditches are always full. The apparatus of the wind-mills
is simple : a number of long broad paddles are fixed in
an axle, the lower ends of which dip into a box of little
more than their own breadth, into which the water of
the lower level flows, and the rapidity with which the
paddles are driven makes them throw the water off
their flat sides, to all the height that is needed. The
country being below the level of the sea, there are
no spring-wells of fresh water in it. The rain that
falls on the roofs of their houses is conveyed into
a cistern, built of brick, sunk in the ground at the side
of the door, or under one of the corners of the house,
and some of them have an opening into the cistern both
within and on the outside of the house. The Dutch
are proverbial for their cleanliness and ingenious industry.
I admired, among other things, their way of churning
their butter. A large wheel, with a broad rim, the
spokes of which were fastened to the one side of the rim,

was fixed upon a nave in the wall, at one of the corners
of the house, with the spokes next to the wall; small
pieces of wood were nailed across the inside of the rim; a
belt that was upon the rim turned a crank that was
above it; the churn stood on the floor under the crank
which lifted the churn staff up and down; there was a
close lid upon the churn, with a slit in the centre, in
which the churn staff moved so much of which was flat,
as allowed it to move in the slit. The wheel was turned
round by a dog, who was put into the inside of the rim
upon the open side, he catched the small cross pieces of
wood, that were on the inside of the fore part of the
rim, at some height, with his feet, and the weight of his
body turned the wheel. The poor dog was tied by a
cord round his neck at such a height to an upright post
at the side of the fore part of the wheel, that if
he did not work he would be hanged. There were
generally two dogs employed, the one relieving the
other.

The Dutchmen wear large small-clothes and cocked
hats; the women wear stays and hoops in their petti-
coats and low crowned broad brimmed straw hats;
but I did not see any that were gaudy, or ragged, in any
part of the country I was in.

On the 10th of Sept. 1799, the enemy, having received accessions to their number, attacked us in our position. It was known to them, that we were shortly to
receive large reinforcements; and they determined to
attack us before these arrived. A strong party attacked the position entrusted to our regiment, which was the
first time that we were in actual action with an enemy.
The dyke sheltered us from their shot; for when they drew
near, we stood on the top of it and fired a volley or two,
which drove them back, and then we sheltered ourselves
from the fire of their artillery by sitting down on the
near side of it. The shot whistled over our heads, and
fell, when its strength was spent, on the ground in our
rear. The enemy was repulsed at all points with loss.
Our regiment's loss was small; one man killed and the
captain of the grenadiers, and three men wounded.
General Moore was also slightly wounded. When the

main body of the enemy retreated, a number of their riflemen remained behind them, under the cover of a house that was near the dyke; one of them came from under the cover, and ran to join the main body; he was instantly fired at I dare say by twenty; yet he got clear off, without any appearance of being hurt. The risk that he ran deterred the remainder from following him, and they surrendered themselves prisoners of war, in number about one hundred.

Shortly after the action of the 10th, a number of troops arrived from England, along with the Duke of York, who took the chief command of the army. A large body of Russian troops also joined us, which increased our number to about thirty-five thousand. And on the 19th Sept. the whole moved forward to attack the enemy. Sir Ralph Abercrombie, with about eight or ten thousand men, of which our brigade was a part, marched the preceding night past the right flank of the enemy, and took the town of Hoorn by surprise. We were now a good way in the rear of the enemy's right, and it was intended that the Duke of York, with the main body of the army, should dislodge the enemy from his positions, and that we should then attack them on their flank and rear, and cut off their retreat.

The Duke was successful at the outset of the action, but the Russians under his command falling into disorder, the enemy rallied upon them, repulsed them, and took a great number of them prisoners, which compelled the Duke to retreat. We heard the firing of the cannon, while we lay on our arms waiting for orders to move, but, when word was brought, that the Duke of York had been driven back, we retired the same way that we came, and were not engaged in this action. We began now to say that we were a lucky regiment; various expressions were used by the soldiers, when speaking of our good luck (as it was called,) some of them very foolish, which I do not mention. Some said, that there were too many old women in Scotland, praying for their children and friends, to allow us to be exposed to great danger. I began to reflect seriously upon our past preservation, and the bad improvement that we were making of it; and the thought made me tremble: I thought, " It *may be*, that God has been more favourable to us than to others; on account of the prayers of godly relatives at home; but his kindness has a claim upon *our gratitude*, and if it does not produce gratitude from *us to him*, he may be provoked to punish us severely, and make his punishment in proportion to his past kindness; and the longer that he bears with us, the stroke may be the heavier when it comes; and although we have as yet escaped more than other regiments, in the next battle it may be, that for hardening ourselves in sin, and flattering ourselves with security, on account of the prayers of godly relatives, we may suffer more severely than any others:"— and my fears were not groundless.

The sand-hills which run along the sea coast from Helder, terminated a little in the rear of Patten, where our right was posted, and commenced again about three miles farther south, in our front. An embankment of sand fills up this breach, and prevents the sea from flowing over the flat country. Tufts of strong straw are set in the sand in regular rows, like plants in a garden, the whole breadth and length of the embankment. The tops of the tufts rise upwards of a foot above the surface of the sand, and the sand that is washed up by the tide or blown by the wind, lodges about their roots and as the tufts are regularly renewed, they not only preserve this bank of light sand from diminishing, but also increase its size and solidity. The left of the enemy's army was posted at the commencement of the sand-hills. It was determined that Sir Ralph Abercrombie, with a division of British troops, should attack the enemy posted there, while the Duke of York, with the other division, of the army, should attack their positions in the flat country. We left our cantonments before one o'clock of the morning of the 2d October, and assembled before day-break on the beach in front of the enemy's lines. At day-break we began to drive in their outposts; and continued to advance along the sea side, while another part of the army advanced along the inland side of the sand-hills, with a line of communication across them. The breadth of the beach along which we advanced was various: (the attack had been several days delayed, on ac-

count of stormy weather, which drove the sea so far upon the beach, as to leave no passage betwixt the sand-
hills and the water) : it admitted sometimes of two or
three companies to march a-breast, and sometimes scarcely of one. We had four pieces of cannon in front, which
fired upon the enemy, who retired along the beach as
we advanced. I passed close by a man, who had been
struck with a cannon ball upon the knee joint; the ball
had carried away the joint, and left a ligament of skin
on each side of it, which held the leg suspended to the
thigh. A little farther, I passed near a man who lay
stretched upon his back, dead ;—his eyes and counten-
nance, had something in them peculiarly dreadful ; yet
he appeared to be only shot through the thigh with a
musket ball:—but it was the centre of it, and it had
proved instantly mortal. I was so struck with this man's
ghastly appearance, that I thought with myself, " Were
I a poet, I would choose, as my subject, the horrors of
war, that I might persuade mankind not to engage in
it."—As we continued to advance, the sand-hills increased in breadth, which required additional troops to fill up
the line of communication across them ; we who remained upon the beach, saw nothing that was doing in the interior of the sand-hills, and as the firing there was only
musketry, the roar of the sea upon the beach, prevented
us from hearing it, except when it was close to us. We
had frequent and long pauses, waiting for the movements
of others. There was a great deal of bloodshed in the
interior of the sand-hills, by the continued skirmishing,
and detached attacks upon particular points. These sand-
hills were admirably adapted for this mode of warfare ;
the enemy would have been much more easily driven out
of trenches ;—for the sand-hills were the same as a succession of trenches, so that when the enemy saw our
troops advancing, they continued to fire upon us until
they saw that we were just near enough to allow them
time safely to retire to the next range of hills. The sand-
hills are not much unlike snow blown into wreaths, by
a strong wind; they are various in their heights and
shapes; some being conical and steep, and others running
in winding ridges; and the sand is so light, as to be carried about with the wind. It is extremely difficult to walk

amongst it, being like dry snow, a little hard on the surface, which when once broken, is almost impassable: here and there, there are chasms, and hollow flats of various extents among them.

Towards the afternoon we drew near a place called Egmont, a small fishing town among the sand-hills, near to where the battle of Camperdown was fought. Here the enemy had drawn a number of fishing sloops and schuyts upon the beach, in two lines, leaving intervals between them, for their troops to pass. These formed a cover to their columns from our shot, and concealed their cavalry from our view. During the action they had received a reinforcement which they pushed along the sand-hills close to the beach. The line across these, owing to their increased breadth, now occupied all the regiments of our division but ourselves. The enemy began to press hard upon the troops that were near us, and so posted themselves as to annoy us who were standing upon the beach; we were a considerable time exposed to this, and had a number both of officers and men wounded, amongst which was Lord Huntly, our Colonel, and a son of Sir Ralph Abercrombie, who was at that time an ensign in the regiment. A situation of this kind is the most irksome for a soldier to be in; for when actively engaged, the fury and bustle of action, to a considerable degree, banishes the dread of danger from the mind.

During the march along the beach, and the frequent pauses we made, my mind had time for serious reflection; I was alive to a sense of present danger; and having no well grounded hope for eternity, should death be the issue, was led to pray earnestly to God for mercy. While standing exposed to the fire of the enemy, and the balls whistling over us and amongst us, my former sins came into my mind, with all my broken vows and resolutions; my past ingratitude stared me in the face, and made me tremble, but a sense of present danger made me pray earnestly for mercy to pardon my sins, and to preserve my life; I confessed that I did not deserve what I sought, but I cast myself on the mercy of God, and with increasing fortitude, as I thought, resolved once more to forsake every sin, and live only to him.—The enemy having increased in numbers, the troops in the sand-hills next to the beach began to give way. Four companies detached from our regiment, with Sir John Moore at their head, went to reinforce them; but they were also soon overpowered; and Sir John was wounded in three parts of the body, and with difficulty escaped being taken prisoner, the remaining six companies were then ordered to form in three divisions, and march forward along the beach, and then to wheel to our left, and charge the enemy. I was in the front division. We marched forward, and passed a number of the enemy's troops, and came to a place where there was a more than ordinary opening, and the sand rose pretty high, in the form of a semicircle; into this opening we wheeled, and were instantly exposed to a fire upon both our flanks and front. This staggered us, and we began to fire upon the enemy, in place of pushing instantly forward to that part of the height that was on our right, driving the enemy from it, and taking up a position there; from which we could have done them more harm, and not have been so much exposed ourselves. We continued to stand still and fire for a few seconds, and then began to move forward, firing as we advanced; the other two divisions had wheeled into various openings in the sand hills in our rear, at the same time that we did. They were strongly opposed by the enemy, who were very superior in number; but hearing the firing of our division in their rear, the enemy who opposed them began to retreat into the interior of the sand-hills; those who opposed us did the same, and we continued to pursue them; but the action soon became on both sides quite irregular; for the sand hills separated us into parties, so that the one party frequently did not see what the other was doing, and, in some instances, parties of our troops came suddenly upon parties of the enemy. In one instance, one of our parties having climbed to the top of a sand ridge, found that a party of the enemy was just beneath, and instantly rushed down the ridge upon them; but the side of the ridge was so steep and soft, that the effort to keep themselves from falling, prevented them from making regular use of their arms. They were involuntarily precipitated amongst the enemy, and the bottom of the ridge was so narrow, and the footing on all sides so soft, that neither party were able, for want of room, to make use of the bayonet; but they struck at each other with the butts of their firelocks, and some individuals were fighting with their fists.—For three quarters of an hour we maintained a furious action, and drove the enemy to a considerable distance; but so many had been killed, and wounded, and scattered, that the officers could no longer collect any great number into one body. We then began to retreat: the enemy turned upon us, and we lost a number of men by their fire during the retreat. Our previous advance had exhausted our bodily strength, and we were much in want of water. I was very thirsty, and began to grow very weak. In the course of the retreat we came to a pretty steep rise of sand. I felt myself unable to go over it, in a straight line; so had to make a circuit, to get over it where it was lower; although it was almost a matter of life and death with me, for a party of the enemy was close behind us. As I was making this circuit, a party, I think in number about six or seven, fired at me all at once, (I was their only object;) and I distinctly observed several balls strike the sand ridge, both before and behind me, about breast high. I really believe that had I been a span-breadth farther forward or backwards from the spot where I at the moment was, there would have been several balls through my body. Before any more fired at me, I got over the ridge, which then secured me; and I joined the regiment, which was near, and had taken up a position in the interior of the sand-hills; and some fresh troops arriving, the enemy was repulsed.

I no doubt had many hair-breadth escapes during the action, of which I was insensible; but the one I have mentioned, appeared to me as a wonderful mercy of Providence, and I looked upon it, as laying me under an additional obligation to devote my whole life to the service of God. If I was bound to serve him, because he was my Creator, I was now doubly bound to serve him, for my wonderful preservation; and I thought that the ties by which I was now bound, would undoubtedly have this effect. I thought I should never indulge in any thing that was sinful; but I was still blind to my own weakness; I had thought the same thing, and had promised accordingly, in prayer to God, at the outset of the action; yet the action was scarcely begun, before I joined my comrades, in furious, opprobrious, and profane language against the enemy. Many sins were thus unobserved by me, and did not affect my conscience at the time.

During the time that we were engaged in the interior of the sand-hills, the enemy, seeing no infantry on the beach to protect our guns, sent out his cavalry, from their covert at Egmont, to seize them. Our cavalry had gone into the chasms of the sand-hills, that were next the beach, a little in the rear, to shelter themselves from the fire of the enemy's cannon. They formed upon the beach, and sprung forward to meet the enemy, who had, by this time, reached the guns. They charged the enemy briskly, and drove them back with considerable loss, and pursued them close to Egmont. But, what is something singular, the infantry parties of French and British, that were on the sand-hills next the beach, suspended, as it were by mutual consent, their firing, to become spectators of the cavalry, and did not commence again until the contest of the cavalry was decided.

The firing ceased sometime before sun-set; I was much in want of water, and went, along with another, to search for it. We found it at last, in the hollow of the opening of the sand-hills, into which we had wheeled when we left the beach and engaged the enemy. There had been a good deal of rain some days before: and the trampling of our feet upon the surface of the sand had brought water to it, which being observed by some who came to the place afterwards, they dug a small hole in the sand, and put into it the sides of an empty broken ammunition box, which served for cradling; and the hole was soon filled with good water. A number more of such kind of wells were presently made, and plenty of water got, which supplied both horse and foot. We filled our canteens; and then went to look among the dead and wounded, for a comrade, of whom we could get no certain account. The spectacle of the dead, the dying, and the wounded, greatly affected me. The dead were lying stiff on the ground, in various postures; but death had so altered their countenances, that of all that I saw, belonging to the regiment, with many of whom I had been familiar, I knew only two; and it was by peculiar marks, such as death could not alter, that we distinguished even them. The groaning of the wounded was very afflicting; for they were mostly bad cases, all that were able to walk or crawl having removed farther to the rear; and all the assistance that could be given to those who were unable to move, was to carry them from the spot where they were lying, to a place of greater shelter. This had been in part already done, and the wounded were lying in groupes, in the best sheltered hollows adjacent to the beach. The universal cry of these poor men was for water. I supplied them as far as I was able, both enemies and friends; and amongst the rest one of our own officers, who was most severely wounded. I had to hold him up and put the canteen to his mouth, for he was unable to help himself; he died during the night. We did not find the object of our search; but we got afterwards certain account of his having been wounded, and probable accounts of his death; and we never heard more of him.

I returned to join the regiment, ruminating on the affecting sight I had seen, and grieved for the loss of comrades and acquaintances. When the regiment was mustered in the evening, about one half were amissing; but about thirty joined in a day or two after, who had lost the regiment. We were upwards of 600 strong; and our loss in killed, wounded, and prisoners (of whom there were 40), was 288. The company to which I belonged, entered the field with 59 rank and file, and three serjeants, out of which 5 were killed on the field, and 24 were wounded, 5 of whom died in a few days, and 3 shortly after. Of the rest, few recovered, so as to be fit for service. The regiment had suffered this severe loss in about three quarters of an hour. There was a universal gloom upon every countenance, when we looked to the smallness of our number, when we were mustered; and there was no one, but what had lost comrades and associates,

E

and some had lost relatives. After it was dark, we planted our picquets, and the remainder of us lay down among
the sand. I reflected upon my own escape—upon the
great number who had already been launched into eternity,
and others whom I had seen groaning under the pain of
wounds, which would soon prove mortal to many of them.
I thanked God for his kindness to me, and promised to
keep his commandments in future.

We lay three days among the sand-hills : the weather
was cold ; the nights stormy and wet. We were waiting for the movements of the other divisions of the army, in the interior of the country. The day after the
battle, we buried such of our dead as were adjacent to
us. One man belonging to the company I was in, was
found dead, without any mark of violence on his body.
He was lying on the ascent of a sand-ridge, and had fallen on the retreat. We conjectured, that fatigue and
want of water had occasioned his death. I was informed of another singular case : A Frenchman and a Highlander had charged upon each other ; the Frenchman
had parried the thrust of the Highlander, and run him
through the body ; the Highlander had then let go his
hold of the butt end of his piece with his right hand, and
seized, with a death-grasp, the throat of the Frenchman ;
who, to extricate himself, had also let go the hold which
he had of his firelock with his right hand, and seized
the wrist of the Highlander, to pull it away from his
throat ; but he had been unable :—the Frenchman had
then staggered backwards, and had fallen on his back ;
and the Highlander above him, still retaining hold of his
throat ; and, in the struggle that had then taken place,
the head of the Highlander had projected so far over
the head of the Frenchman, as to bring that part of the
body of the former in which the bayonet was, over the
mouth of the latter ; and in this posture both had ex-
pired. Those who saw it, said, the sight was truly shocking. The Frenchman was fairly strangled ; his eyes
were out of their sockets ; his tongue was greatly
swelled, and thrust far out of his mouth, into which
the blood from the wound of the Highlander was running. Each still held a firm hold of his firelock with his

left hand; and when the Highlander was removed from the Frenchman, and laid along-side of him, he still kept such a firm grasp of his throat, that he raised the body of the Frenchman from the ground, and it was with difficulty it was extricated from the hold.

The result of the battle of the 2d October compelled the enemy to abandon his positions, and evacuate the town of Alkmaar, which was his head quarters, and fall back nearer to Amsterdam. Alkmaar was occupied by our troops on the 3d, and as our brigade had been much reduced in number, we were ordered to go there to form a part of its intended garrison. The peninsula is here of considerable breadth, and the country much superior to that on the north side of the long dyke, but it is still intersected with deep broad ditches and canals, which greatly impede military operations. The rain that had lately fallen had filled the canals and ditches so full of water, that the edges and lower parts of the roads were beginning to be covered, as we passed from Egmont to Alkmaar; and as the roads, for want of stone, were made of earth, or a slight layer of sand upon earth or clay, they were beginning to be deep. There are narrow foot-paths laid with brick, between some of the towns. Alkmaar is a town of considerable size, surrounded with a high mound of earth and a canal; all the entrances to it are over draw-bridges and through gates, the principal of which have cannon mounted on them. The streets are paved with whinstone in the centre, and on the sides with brick or flags, and a number of large canals run through the centre of the principal of them.

We entered the town on the 5th, and next day, which was Sunday, the garrison was taken to the church, to attend divine service. The Dutch congregation had been dismissed; but their minister, and a number of others, remained, to be a witness of our service. The church was large, and of Gothic structure, and had the largest and most highly ornamented organ I ever saw. The enemy had received reinforcements the day before, and he commenced an attack upon the positions of the army, at the time we were in the church. The prayers of the liturgy had been read, and the minister had begun his sermon, when we began to hear the noise of cannon at a distance ; by the time the sermon was ended, the firing of cannon had approached nearer the town, and was beginning to be heavy, and the musketry was heard to mingle in the roar ; and the large organ played Malbrouk as we left the church, to repair to our alarm ports. The action continued to be warmly contested, until after it was dark ; but the enemy was repulsed, and fell back to his position, and one hundred and eighty-eight prisoners were taken, and brought into Alkmaar on the morning of the 7th.

About two o'clock in the afternoon the prisoners were assembled, and a captain and forty men, of whom I was one, were appointed to escort them to our former head-quarters, on the north side of the long dyke. Only thirty of the prisoners were French ; the others were Dutchmen, and had put up the orange cockade after they were made prisoners. Numbers of them had money, with which they procured gin before we left the town ; and they drank and sung songs (which we believed were in praise of their former government), as we went along the road. The Frenchmen, who were enthusiastic republicans, scorned the Dutch for putting up the orange cockade, and kept by themselves, on the front of the party. We kept them all in good humour, and until the fatigue of travelling had exhausted our strength, the march of the prisoners resembled more the merry air of a wedding procession, than of that gloom which the thought of their being under an escort of their enemies, and on the way to a prison in a foreign land, might naturally be expected to produce. It continued to rain upon us the greater part of the way, this, with the deepness of the roads and the length of the journey, fatigued us exceedingly, and scattered us into parties ; yet, notwithstanding of this, and although a great part of the journey was performed after it was dark, and although the prisoners were in their own country, none of them attempted to escape. When we had delivered them over to another guard, to watch them through the night, we retired to rest in the expectation of returning to Alkmaar next day, but we were surprised to hear in the morning, that the army was retreating ; and in a few hours, the various divisions arrived and resumed the positions they had occupied previous to the battle of the 2d.

The reasons of this retrograde movement were the badness of the roads from Helder to the interior. The army received its bread from the fleet, and all the ammunition and military stores; the roads were becoming impassable, and the farther we advanced, the difficulties of fetching our supplies from the Helder were increasing. The French armies in Switzerland, and on the Rhine, had gained decisive victories, which enabled them to detach large bodies of troops, which were on their way, to re-enforce their army in Holland, which would then become so strong as to be able to overpower us. It had, therefore, been determined to retreat while the roads were passable, lest our retreat might be cut off. The army retired from all its positions early in the morning, and the rear guard left Alkmaar early in the day. The enemy, after being repulsed on the 6th, was apprehensive that we might attack him, and was prepared, in that case, to retire to Haarlem; our retreating was not expected by him, and it was about 10 o'clock in the forenoon before his advanced cavalry picquets discerned that Alkmaar was evacuated, when they entered and found a few drunken women and soldiers, whose intoxication prevented them from knowing that the army had retreated. In a few days after the retreat of the army, an armistice was agreed upon, the conditions of which were, that we should evacuate Holland by the end of November, and release eight thousand prisoners without exchange, as a boon for our being allowed quietly to re-embark. This agreement put an end to hostilities, and preparations were made to send home the troops with all possible expedition; but, before we left the country, I caught the ague, and after we had arrived in England, in the beginning of November, 1799, I was put into the hospital in Chelmsford, twenty-six miles from London. I was greatly reduced in body before I recovered, which was not until the beginning of the next year, 1800.—God's mercy in granting me a recovery from the ague, impressed my mind with the additional obligations I was now laid under to serve him:—but, as formerly, my re-

solutions of mind were soon broken ; conscience soon
found matter of accusation against me ; I was at times
careless and listless, and at other times thoughtful and
pensive.   The barracks in which we lay, were about a
mile from the town of Chelmsford.   There was a tabernacle in the town, where there was sermon once a fortnight in the evening.   I went several times to it ; and
the sermons served to awaken my religious impressions.
One evening, the preacher described a case of conscience,
which I thought not unlike my own; and among other
directions, he exhorted the person who might be in such
a case, to lay it before God in prayer.   After the service was over, I shunned my companions ; returned to
the barracks alone, and prayed to God for light and direction as I went along the road ; and I set about reforming
my conduct once more.   But I soon fell through it, and
was thrown as far back as ever.——There were no religious meetings in the regiment, from the time we left Ireland until a good while after this.

CHAPTER IV.

We left Chelmsford on the 14th of April, and marched to the Isle of Wight, where we lay until the 27th May.
I was once in the Methodist meeting-house while we
lay in the town of Newport.   On the 27th May, 1800,
we embarked on board the Diadem, 64 guns, and the
Inconstant frigate, both armed *en flute* (*i. e.* partially
armed), and fitted for the reception of troops.   We left
all our women and heavy baggage in the Isle of Wight;
and as we were not informed where we were going, this
circumstance led us to conjecture, that we were destined
for some desperate and secret enterprize.   We were
joined by some more ships with troops, and sailed down
the English channel, until we fell in with the Channel
fleet, under the command of Sir John Jarvis.   Sir Ed-
ward Pellew, (now Lord Exmouth,) was sent along
with us, with a squadron of eight ships of war.   It was
a magnificent sight to see the Channel fleet in regular

1

order. They were in number forty-four ships of the
line, (a large proportion of them three-deckers) and
a number of frigates. We sailed along the coast of
France until we came to the bay of Quiberon, where we
came to an anchor on the 2d June, near a small island
called Houet, lying betwixt the isle of Belleisle and the
main land, about four or five miles from the latter, and
six or seven from Belleisle.

On the 4th, which was the anniversary of his Majesty's
birth, a singular occurrence took place. A sloop of war,
and a number of boats armed with carronades, having
detachments of troops in them, were despatched in the
morning, to attack a battery situated on a projecting
point of the main land, where it approaches nearest to
Belleisle, and from which ships coming to our present
anchorage, were liable to be fired upon. It lay about
eight or ten miles from us: but as the wind was light,
the sloop of war and the boats did not get near the battery, until it was past twelve o'clock. The battery then
opened a fire from two 24-pounders, which played briskly upon them. The day was fine and clear, which permitted us to see the smoke of every gun that was fired,
and where the shot struck the water. We looked on
with eager anxiety, and observed all the movements
of the sloop of war and the boats. It was near one
o'clock before she was in a position to return the fire of
the battery, which she did briskly. The armed boats
then pulled towards the shore, under cover of her fire.
At one o'clock they were close to the battery, and commenced a smart fire upon it from their carronades, and
the contest was at the hottest, just at the instant that
the ships we were in, were firing the salute in honour
of his Majesty's birth day. The enemy precipitately
retired from the battery, and the troops and seamen
landed, dismounted the guns, broke the carriages, and
did what other damage they could, and then returned
to the fleet. We all remarked the singularity of the circumstance, that while we were saluting with blank shot,
they were saluting with round, double headed, and grape
shot, in real earnest, by which several lives were lost,
and some were wounded, besides other damages.

We landed on the island of Houet on the 6th June. It was a small place, almost destitute of cultivation, and only a little fishing village on it. Some more ships arrived from England with troops, and preparations were made for attacking Belleisle. On the 15th June, we were embarked on board the ships of the line, in order to go near the island, and make our debarkation from them, under the cover of their guns. Our regiment was wholly on board of the Terrible, 74. We were five days in this ship; and here there were a number of the sailors, who were serious, and united together for prayer and praise; some of them were known to several of our men; the seamen were all very kind, and uncommonly obliging to us; every thing was orderly and quiet; religion appeared to have so far prevailed in this ship, as to give a general tone to the manners and conversation of the seamen; so that they were not like the same kind of men that we met with in other ships of war. Those men who were not religious, did not make a mock at religion; and those who were serious, were in the habit of having what might be called public prayers between decks, at stated periods. This was intimated through the ship, by two or more individuals going round and informing the sailors that there were to be prayers at such a gun, say, No. 9 or 10, on the starboard or larboard side. At these public meetings, I understood, that one or other of them addressed their fellow seamen. In these practices they appeared to be protected by their officers; and they held a meeting for prayer and praise, on the forecastle, evening and morning: I had some conversation with some of them who were natives of Scotland; but I was never actually present at any of the meetings. We were so crowded, that it was with difficulty we could move from one part of the ship to another; and we durst never be any time absent from the place where our arms were, lest we should lose them, and not find them readily, as we were under orders to be at a moment's notice to go into the boats. Our coming to this ship, was one of the steps of divine providence for my good; for seeing and hearing something of religion in it, awakened once more in my heart, a concern for my soul; and, although it wore off, as before, it was a means of preventing me from becoming confirmed in a state of careless indifference.

On the 18th June, the Captain, 74, while under sail, happened to approach the shore, and went within reach of shot. When she put about, to stand out from the shore, she was fired upon from several points nearly in the same instant, and received some damage before she got out of reach. The batteries which fired upon her were concealed from view; and we were informed, that the shore was defended by batteries, at all the points where it was convenient to land. We were waiting for the arrival of some more troops from England, which were hourly expected, but did not arrive. —On the 20th, the enterprize was given up. It was said that, during the hazy weather, which had prevented us from seeing to any distance, re-enforcements had been sent into Belleisle. We returned to the isle of Houet, and to our tents, which had been left standing. Our number was said to be about 5000. On the next day, orders arrived for us to embark, which was done; and we sailed on the day following under sealed orders, and left the ships of war that belonged to the Channel fleet.

We had a pleasant and quick passage to the Straits of Gibraltar, where our Commodore informed us, that we were destined for the island of Minorca, to join an expedition that was forming under Sir Ralph Abercrombie, to assist the Austrians in Italy. We passed through the Straits, but did not touch at Gibraltar. We arrived at Minorca on the 21st July. We then learned, that Sir Ralph Abercrombie had already been at Leghorn; but that the Austrians having sustained a severe defeat from the French, under Buonaparte, had made an agreement, which did not allow of British troops being landed, and that Sir Ralph had brought back what troops he had to Minorca. We landed for refreshment and exercise on the 7th of August, and the whole regiment embarked again, on the 30th, on board of the Stately, 64. We sailed on the 31st for Gibraltar, where we arrived on the 14th September. We were there

joined by another expedition, under the command of
Sir James Pulteney. They had sailed from England in
the beginning of July, and had made a descent on the
coast of Spain at Ferrol, but had not effected any thing,
except alarming the country. There was now a large
body of troops on board this fleet; their number being
about 25,000. There were in all, upwards of 100 sail
of large ships; two-thirds of which were war vessels of
one description or other We were in want of water,
to get which, we went to Tetuan bay, which is on the
Barbary shore, to the south-east of Gibraltar, belonging
to Morocco. Here the whole fleet completed their
stores of provisions and water. We set sail on the 27th,
with an intention to pass the straits of Gibraltar; but
the wind changed, and after ating about, we put back
to Tetuan on the 29th. On the 1st October, the wind
having become fair, we set sail, passed through the
Straits, and anchored next day near to Cadiz in Spain.
On the 3d of October we got orders to be in readiness
to land. A flag of truce came from the shore to the
Admiral on the 4th, and returned back the same day.
On the 6th, the day being fine, we weighed anchor and
stood across the bay of Cadiz, with the intention of
landing near the town of St. Mary's. The dispositions having been made for landing, the ships of war,
intended to cover the debarkation, were moving towards
the shore, and a cutter had gone so near as to be fired
upon. The first division of troops were in the boats, and
had rowed off for the shore : we were all in readiness,
and were receiving our ammunition; I had just got mine
in six parcels, of ten cartridges each, when a flag of truce,
which we had seen coming from the harbour, reached
the Admiral's ship; and before I had got the half of the
cartridges into my pouch, a signal was made by the Admiral, for the boats to return, and put the troops on
board their respective ships, the design of landing being
relinquished.—We were struck with the suddenness of
the change. The flag of truce returned to the shore;
and a report was spread, that the place had been ran-
somed by money; but whether there was any truth in
this, or whether any political concession had been made,

cannot be known. There was one thing, however, and possibly it might be the only thing that prevented our landing; the plague was raging in Cadiz at the time.

I have been somewhat minute in detailing this circumstance; but it has always appeared to me, a very striking occurrence in Providence; for, in a very few minutes, the war vessels would have opened their broadsides upon the troops and batteries on the shore; the troops in the boats would soon have been under the enemy's fire, and probably have effected a landing; and, if hostilities had once commenced, it is difficult to tell, but the enterprize might have been pushed, until Cadiz had been taken, and their fleet of war-ships captured or destroyed, unless the Spanish force had been too strong for us.

This event once more awakened me, by a sense of apparent danger. The prospect of having to contend with what troops might be in the field, and of having to attack fortified places, and the likelihood, that desperate efforts would be made to gain our purpose, before the Spaniards should have time to collect a large force in the field, made me apprehend that the undertaking was one of no ordinary danger. My conduct on this occasion, was similar to what it had been on former occasions. I prayed for mercy and preservation. I still had no hope for eternity, but what was to arise out of future reformation of character, a reformation which was yet to begin. As formerly, I now again resolved to set about it:—but we left the bay of Cadiz on the 7th, and returned to Tetuan bay on the 12th, and part of the fleet put into Gibraltar: and the danger I had dreaded being thus past, the resolution it had excited was soon departed from.

But another danger of a different kind, was at hand. On the 15th, the north-east wind had risen to a great height, so that our boats, which had gone with empty casks to get water, were obliged to return to the ship and leave their casks on shore; and the storm kept increasing as the evening drew on. At 8 o'clock at night the splice of our cable slipped, and we began to drift.

As we had only one other anchor on board, which was not sufficient to ride the storm with, we endeavoured to put to sea. It was at a great risk that we effected this. We were in the midst of a large fleet, and were every moment in danger of running foul of one or other of the ships. With difficulty we got the fore-sail, and some of the stay-sails set, and, although the night was very dark, by the goodness of God, we got clear out from the fleet, and steered for Gibraltar. When we came there, as we passed by the stern of the Admiral's ship, we were ordered to pass through the Straits, and anchor on the west side of Barbary. We accordingly put about, and passed through the Straits before the wind, going at the rate of seven miles an hour, under our bare poles. We had a large flat-bottomed boat at our stern, which the stormy weather did not permit us to hoist on board; and by daylight in the morning, there was nothing of it remaining but the keel with the ring bolt, by which it was towed. Before day-break we had cleared the Straits of Gibraltar. We then set some sail, and stood off and on the Barbary coast, until the 17th, when, the weather moderating, we cast anchor. On the 18th, the weather cleared up, and we perceived a number of the fleet at anchor to windward of us, nearer the shore, at about 20 miles distance. We weighed anchor and beat to windward to join them; but the weather again got squally, and about one o'clock a squall overtook us, which carried away our main-top, and top-gallant, and mizen topgallant masts. We shortly after came to anchor near the fleet, and the weather becoming moderate, in the course of next day, we got our damages pretty well repaired, and received an additional anchor from the Ajax man of war. On the 23d we set sail; passed once more through the Straits of Gibraltar; anchored in Tetuan bay for the third time on the 26th; and after having completed our water, and received some more provisions, we sailed on the 8th Nov. for Minorca, to get our provisions and other ship stores completed.

We now began to hear that we were bound for Egypt. At this we were all very sorry, not knowing when we might return, or who might have the happiness of seeing their native country again. I had often read and heard of the dangerous nature of the climate of Egypt, and of the disasters of the French army there by the plague. The prospect now before us made a strong impression on my mind. I became more serious; religion began to be more attended to by several, and a party for prayer and conversation was formed; but I was not one of the number, being too proud to associate with them.

We made the island of Minorca on the 16th; but the wind being strong and contrary, we did not get into the harbour until the 21st, and having obtained what we wanted, we set sail again on the 27th for Malta, where we arrived on the 6th December. The day we made the island was very fine, and as Malta was a place of note on various accounts, and amongst others, as being the place where the apostle Paul suffered shipwreck, I staid upon deck, from the time we came in sight of it, which was in the morning, until we were anchored in the harbour. As we sailed along the island, I anxiously looked for the "*place where two seas met.*" As we passed by the small island of Comena, the *creek* where the apostle says they thrust in the ship, was easily discerned. It bears now the name of St. Paul's bay, and the channels between Comena, Goza, and Malta, meet at it, which marks it as the place which Paul describes.

We left Malta on the 21st, and sailed for Marmorice bay in Asia. In our voyage, we coasted along the whole length of the south side of the island of Candia, which is ancient Crete, after which we came to the isle of Rhodes, which is only about 20 miles distant from the coast of Asia. I felt a more than usual interest in looking at those places, from what I had read of them in history, particularly from what is said of them in the Scriptures. Little did I think, in reading of them when a boy, that I should one day see them, or that I should do the duty of a soldier in the land of Egypt.

From Rhodes we steered direct for the opposite coast of Asia, and, entering into a passage of some length, between two high hills, we wondered where we were going, for we did not see any place in this opening fit for ships to lie in, and the land on both sides was rocky hills, covered

F

with wood, (except where the rocks were completely bare of soil,) and appeared to be the habitations of wild beasts. When we arrived very near the head of the inlet, we were surprised to see a ship that was a little ahead of us, get out of our sight almost in an instant; but when we had got a little farther, we found a passage which turned to the right, round a very perpendicular hill, as suddenly as if it had been the corner of a street. Into this passage we sailed. It was but short, and in a few minutes we entered into one of the largest and finest bays, it is said, in the world. Here we cast anchor on the 29th Dec. 1800, and lay until the 23d Feb. 1801, making arrangements for our attacking the French in Egypt; procuring horses for the use of the artillery and cavalry: and cutting wood for fuel, and for making fascines and pallisades, in case they should be needed after we landed. The bay is nearly surrounded with high hills, which, except in and about the small town of Marmorice, are covered with wood, in general very thick. There are great numbers of wild beasts in the woods, which make so much noise in the night time, as to be heard over the whole bay. There was a small plain on one side of the bay, where we pitched tents for those that were sick; but there was a necessity to have a guard, to keep on fires in the rear of the tents, during the night; and some nights the noise of the wild beasts indicated their being so near the tents, that the sentinels fired to keep them at a distance. Some seamen belonging to one of the war ships, who were cutting wood at one place, ventured to stay all night on the shore; they were killed by the wild beasts before morning.

We were not long in this place, until a market was erected on shore, and vessels from the adjacent coast soon found their way to it, with all kinds of fruit, and sheep and goats, and other useful articles; so that that part of the shore assumed the appearance of one of our country fairs. The soil around the bay is to all appearance fertile; but cultivation has been on the decline for a long time past, which has allowed the wood to extend, in several places, to the very shores. At some distant period, the shores seem to have been better peopled, and the wood to have been farther back. I found the ruins of a house

1

upon the top of a small eminence, pretty far back in the woods. The walls were partly standing; trees were growing out of the floor; a plot of ground, which had been levelled for a garden, still retained its shape, and had a fine spring of water running through it. Land turtle is in plenty in the woods.

I shall now return, to state what were the exercises of my mind, during the passage up the Mediterranean, and while we lay in this bay.—A book upon the first principles of astronomy fell in my way. This gave me a new view of creation: and at the same time a treatise on Philology came into my hands, in which was a descant on the glory of God in the works of nature. I had undergone some very sharp convictions of sin, my mind had been strongly impressed with eternal things, and I had persuaded two of my comrades to join with me in prayer; which we did on several occasions, but fell off from it. After reading the above-mentioned books, and several volumes of the Spectator, my mind fell into a strange speculative frame, on the duty of the creature to glorify its Creator, let the Creator do what he will to the creature. I reasoned thus with myself:—That every thing that God did was wise and just, therefore it was our duty to glorify God for all that he did to us, whether it was in judgment or in mercy: did he deal with us in mercy—gratitude ought to lead us to glorify him; did he deal with us in judgment—it was our own sins that provoked him to do it: he did no more than what was just; and we were as really bound to glorify him for his justice, as for his mercy; and if we did not do so, we augmented our guilt. By reasoning in this way, I came at last to a fallacious and very dangerous conclusion, under the guise of wisdom. I concluded, that if I could not lessen what guilt was already contracted, neither altogether avoid contracting more, it would be wise to contract as little additional guilt as possible ; and that, should God deal with me in justice, I must not complain and murmur; he is holy, just, and wise ; he will not punish me above what I deserve ; whatever he does with me, his creature, it becomes me to glorify his name, by a cheerful acquiescence in his divine procedure ; yea to glorify

Him, should I be for ever damned. By doing this, I may possibly make hell more tolerable than otherwise it would be: if I cannot escape his justice, by his not granting me mercy, let me behave in such a manner, as may make the consequences of his wrath sit the lighter upon me.— I shudder to think on this part of my experience at this day; on the pain of mind with which it was accompanied, and the fallacious and dangerous opiate, which the conclusion contained to lull my conscience asleep; for I did in consequence fall into a careless and listless state of mind. But, by the goodness of God, I was not allowed to remain long under it. It happened one day shortly after, that, from eating salt provisions, and from the extreme scantiness of water, I became exceedingly thirsty, and with great difficulty procured a little to drink. A thought then shot across my mind :—if I am so impatient under a temporary thirst, and so eager to procure relief, how shall I preserve my patience in hell?—if I am so unhappy under the pressure of so trivial a circumstance, how much more unhappy shall I be, if I be cast into everlasting burnings, where I shall not have one drop of water to cool my tongue! This broke the delusion, but it did not eradicate it.

An infectious fever broke out among us. It was at first slow in its progress, but after a short time it began to infect numbers. Our condition on board the Stately contributed towards it; for we had no hammocks, nor beds, but only our camp blankets to sleep in; we lay upon the under deck, and, when the weather was stormy, so much water leaked in by the edges of the ports, as made the lee side of the ship very wet. When she tacked, the water that was lying in the lee side would then run across the whole deck; and although we dried it the best way we could, yet we were so crowded that we were often under the necessity of lying down upon the damp deck. This was hurtful to us, causing us to feel stiff, and our bones sore; and although it did not *produce* the fever, (for it was introduced by some recruits who came on board at Malta,) it was, in my opinion, one cause of its spreading so rapidly at last.

I caught this fever at the time it began to spread, and

it was pretty severe upon me. I got better, and relapsed, and the second turn of it was worse than the first.* While under it, I had time to consider myself more fully. My present condition was so painful, that I would have done all in my power, and given all I could possess, to be free from it; and yet with my most sanguine hopes, I could not expect hell to be one half so tolerable. What, thought I, is the glory of God, to me as a creature? If that same glory only renders me miserable, will the misery of my condition, if I am sent to hell, be in any measure alleviated, by the consideration, that the justice of God is glorified by my condemnation? It is true, I shall not cease to exist; but what pleasure can I have in my existence, unless I reap some benefit by it, by having some portion of happiness in it? If I am made completely miserable, and have no prospect of any portion of happiness for the future, my existence must prove my greatest misery. He who knows all things has said, " Good were it for that man, if he had never been born." If the justice of God dooms me to suffer for my sins, woe is me! I now exist, and I cannot annihilate myself: nor can I fly from God's justice. I am a sinner, and if I receive not mercy, I must be for ever miserable! How awful is his justice! How great is his power! How daring and delusive the thought of hoping to find any portion of happiness in that place, where he has declared all is perfect misery; where nothing dwells but the terrors of the Almighty; where the subjects of his justice are a terror to themselves, and to each other; where there is nothing but weeping, and wailing, and gnashing of teeth!

As I began to recover, I turned my thoughts, more closely than before, to those places of Scripture which describe hell, the place of torment. I examined what the Scripture has said of its awful nature; that it is " a fearful thing to fall into the hands of the living God;"— for " who knoweth the power of his anger?" and " our God is a consuming fire." I found, also, that the Scrip-

* There were few of the regiment that escaped it; all relapsed after the first recovery, and those who were longest of catching the infection were worst.

ture evidence of its being endless in its duration, was as conclusive as that of the endless duration of the happiness of heaven. He who said that the one was eternal, said the same of the other. But, when contemplating this awful subject, I was at times tempted to think, " It may be, that although God has said so, he may not intend to execute his dreadful threatening to the full extent : there may be a future period, in which he will extend mercy to his creatures, but which he has kept hid from them, for wise purposes, that they might not presume on his mercy, and spend their present lives in sin, and not repent in this world, because their would be an opportunity to repent in the next."—But this reasoning did not long deceive me ; for I continued to ponder the subject, and I saw that such a notion did not consist with the veracity of God. He could not say one thing, while he intended another ; if I admitted that he said one thing and intended another, with respect to the duration of punishment in hell, it would, with equal consistency, apply to what he said of the endless happiness of heaven, and so render uncertain any hope that might be built upon the promise of it ; and if the principle were in one case admitted, it would throw loose all his promises and threatenings, respecting both this world and the next ; for we should still have room to think, God has said so, but he does not mean so.—I also reflected, if God has said, that the punishment of hell shall be eternal, and has a secret purpose of mercy at some distant period, if this is a secret of his own, how can any one know it ? If he has not told it, how is it possible for any one to find out that which God intends should be secret ? Reflection upon this idea, put an end to the speculation, as being a gross absurdity. I also reflected on the nature of sin ;—I said to myself, " Supposing I were cast into hell for the sins of my present life, would I cease to commit sin when there ? and if I did what was in itself sinful in hell, would the torments of the place excuse it ? would the justice of God take no cognizance of what I did there ?" This was a piercing exercise to my mind : but it was salutary ; and I believe I was indebted to what I had read in Boston's Fourfold State for it, although I was not

aware of it at the time. I answered the above queries in
this way: If, when I am in a state of partial sufferings
here, I am not able to suffer without being at least impatient and fretful, if I do not actually complain and
murmur—how can I expect to behave any better in
hell? My present sufferings do not excuse the sins I
commit under them; I shall then, as well as now, be a
subject of the justice of God; and when I shall be suffering for past sins, that will be no excuse for the commission of new ones; if I am to make the debt of sin less
by suffering for it, I must not contract more debt at the
time I am paying the old; for if I do, I shall continue to
be a debtor; and as long as I continue to commit sin, I
must continue to suffer for it, for the claims of Divine
justice are indispensible.   Following out these reflections
put a complete end to all speculation, of the probability,
or possibility, of ever finding any portion of happiness, if
I did not obtain the pardon of my sins, and deliverance
from sin itself, before I left this world, and appeared in
the presence of God.—These speculations show, that my
mind was ready to catch at any thing, that appeared to
furnish the least hope, however delusive it might be;
for when I looked forward to eternity, not having the
confidence that arises from faith in the Lord Jesus, as
an all-sufficient Saviour, and not discerning the doctrine
of his complete atonement, and justifying righteousness,
I was glad to lay hold of any thing that appeared to af-
ford the smallest glimpse of hope, rather than be without
hope altogether.

Having, by the goodness of God, recovered from the
fever, the effect of it was to make me resolve once more
to devote myself to his service.   Gratitude for his mercy
in my recovery induced me to do this; and I hoped for
better success in my endeavours than heretofore: but
alas! it was not long before my conscience found matter
of accusation against me; and this threw me as far back
as ever.   I searched for a reason why I failed in my at-
tempts to serve God; but I did not find the true one.   I
began to lay the blame on the example and conversation
of my comrades; and would fain have palliated the evil

of my conduct on this ground, and have flattered myself that God would therefore be the less strict with me. But then I reflected, that it would be a pernicious and fatal delusion for me, to flatter myself with any thing that would not stand the test of his judgment seat. I found no toleration for sin, in any situation, in the word of God; and my conscience charged me, not only with wilful sins, for which I could devise no excuse, but also with loving sin itself, which God hateth. Yet, as experience had taught me that one thing led to another, I determined to keep myself as much as possible out of the company of the profligate, and profane, and loose talkers, and to keep my mind as constantly fixed as possible on serious subjects. I set heaven with all its charms before my mind, as the object to be gained, and hell with all its terrors as the object to be escaped. I contrasted time with eternity, and said to myself, Surely eternity is of such vast importance, as to be worth all the sufferings that can be endured, and all the exertions that can be made, in the narrow bounds of human life. I again set out in a new course of obedience, resolved to watch all the avenues to temptation; and, under the influence of this resolution, I avoided, as much as I could, in my present situation, those whose conversation I wished to shun; but it was impossible to be always out of the hearing of it;—all I could do, was not to mingle in converse with them; and I have frequently stopped my ears with my fingers, that I might not hear licentious and profane talk, when I knew it was going on: but I could not do this on every occasion, and when I did get it done, it gave me a proof of the deceitfulness of my own heart; for evil thoughts and sinful desires would spring up in it even at the time when I was stopping my ears, that I might not hear the wicked conversation of others. To this, however, I was not sufficiently attentive, but laid the blame, in some shape or other, on the temptations with which I was surrounded, as being, either directly or indirectly, the cause why I was not able to keep my own heart. This led me to despair of my ever being able to serve God aright, and obtain his favour, by keeping his commandments, while I remained in the army. I therefore began to wish I were free of it, and placed in a situation where I should have it in my power to enjoy solitude and keep out of the way of temptation. I thought that of a hermit a very favourable one; not that I wished to be a hermit altogether, but I fancied if I were only in a situation in which I could keep myself, in a great measure, secluded from the world, and give myself to reading, meditation, and devotion, I should then serve God in a perfect manner. Here again I began to reflect—What, if God cuts me off for my sins while I am in the army? What shall become of me? Have I any hope, if I should die, or be slain, while in the army? To this perplexing question I could give no answer; all I could do, was to pray to God to spare my life, to deliver me from the army, and to bring me into a situation in which I should have it in my power to serve him. But my mind soon misgave me, and led me to suspect that this was not right; and on examining it, I became convinced that I was equally bound to serve God in my present situation as in any other. Our Lord's answer to Paul's prayer, " My grace is sufficient for thee," and many other promises of God to his people came into my mind; and, although I did not understand them aright, yet they convinced me that my situation would not be an excuse for my sins; they convinced me, that if I was one of God's children, his grace would be sufficient to enable me to serve him acceptably, whatever situation his providence might allot me. But knowing, at the same time, that bad company had a great effect in confirming evil habits, I still thought, that were I but free of the army, I should have a great deal less to struggle with. Before I was free of the army, however, experience convinced me that solitude was no antidote to a deceitful heart; for in the solitary hours of night, while watching and on guard, and during the sleepless nights passed in the hospital, I found abundance of sinful thoughts and desires arise in my heart.

I next went to the opposite extreme, and imagined a state of unremitting activity was the best. I thought that were I discharged and at home, I should then enjoy the means of grace on the Sabbath; that my work would occupy my mind the greater part of my time through the week ; and that I should then have it in my power so to regulate my conduct, as to take up my whole attention between lawful and serious things, and thus leave no vacant room in my mind for evil thoughts or what might lead me to the commission of sin.

Under these exercises of mind I continued until the time when we left Marmorice Bay, which was on the 23d February, 1801, when the fleet weighed anchor, and were all safely collected upon the coast, outside of the bay, before sun set, and then steered their course for Egypt. A Turkish Admiral, with two or three frigates, had joined the fleet. A number of Greek vessels also were with us, which had been hired to transport the horses that had been procured at Marmorice, for the use of the artillery, cavalry, and field officers. The wind was brisk, but the evening was fine, and as our fleet consisted of near two hundred sail, many of which were large and elegant ships, it had a grand and interesting appearance. This interest was heightened by the consideration of the sea, and the coast, that we were sailing on, for the celebrated island of Rhodes was on our right, and the coast of Asia Minor on our left. The various nations on board of this fleet, as seamen and soldiers, was novel and striking, for there were Turks, Greeks, and English, with Corsicans, and a brigade of soldiers in our service, composed of men from various parts of Germany, but the part that the soldier was destined to act in the enterprise before us, was to him the most interesting contemplation, for his personal safety was the most deeply involved in the undertaking. The wind continued to freshen, and " the fleet had not stood long on its course before one of the Greek vessels, laden with mules, foundered, and one man alone was saved." The Turkish frigates and Greek vessels left us, and took shelter in the nearest ports. The weather was not what we considered bad, but they were not good navigators : their departure, however, was a serious loss to the army, for the want of the horses on board of them. The weather became moderate, and on the 28th we fell in with our squadron that was blockading Alexandria, and on the

1st March discovered land somewhat to the westward of that place. The wind had been light through the day, but freshened during the night, and there were heavy showers of rain. This made the soldiers remark, That if there was no rain in Egypt, there was rain very near it: some who were of a deistical turn began to insinuate that the Bible had not given a correct account of Egypt; and the apparent contradiction made some of us rather at a loss to reconcile it. During the course of conversation on this subject, I heard one observe, that the Bible did not say directly that there never was any rain in Egypt, but that when it spoke of there being no rain there, it referred to the agriculture of Egypt, not depending, like that of other countries, upon rain, but upon the annual inundations of the Nile.* This is the fact; but it is also true, that although during the winter season there are thunder storms and rain on the sea-coast, yet these seldom go far into the country, and at Grand Cairo rain is a great rarity. After the regiment had been at that city and returned, and after we left Egypt, having staid in it six months, I never heard any one urge the objection any more. All agreed that the scripture account of Egypt was as true as general expressions could describe it; so that this, like many other infidel objections, was founded on an apparent, not a real contradiction. The universal remark upon the country was, that they believed a remnant of the plagues of Moses still existed in it.

CHAPTER V.

On the forenoon of the 2d March, we cast anchor in Aboukir Bay, the place where the battle of the Nile was fought. Here we lay until the 8th, before the weather would permit us to land; a period of great anxiety, for every hour was giving the enemy time to collect his forces, and prepare the means of defence. This made the

* Zech. xiv. 18. Deut. xi. 10. and connection.

prospect increasingly awful. Our regiment was intended to have been one of those which should land first;
but the fever having increased so much, that about one
half of our number were at this time sick, we were unfit to perform a regiment's part, and another of equal
strength was put in our place. The bay was shallow,
and the ships which contained the troops being in general of a large size, had to anchor at a considerable
distance from the shore. On the 7th, a number of
smaller vessels which had been loaded with provisions,
but whose cargoes were now nearly expended, were
moved to about three miles from the shore; and several
regiments were put on board of them, that support might
be quickly given to those who landed first. All of our
regiment fit for duty were ordered into one of these
vessels in the evening. The weather was now favourable,
and every thing indicated that the landing would be attempted next morning. I slept little or none during the
night; but frequently employed myself in short prayers
to God to be merciful to me, and to spare me and protect me from danger.—I was surprised this night with a
want of my ordinary sight, and heard numbers of my
comrades say that they did not see so well as usual, and
yet they had no pain in their eyes.

About two o'clock in the morning the signal was made
for the first division of the troops to get into the boats,
and at three o'clock they were ordered to row for their
rendezvous in the rear of one of the light-war vessels that
was anchored about a gun-shot from the shore. This
was a very fatiguing service to the seamen; because the
fleet was so widely anchored, and many of the large ships
so far from the shore, that it was nine o'clock before they
were all collected and arranged. The enemy could see
all our movements; and the unavoidable delays that took
place, gave them a fair opportunity to provide for their
defence, for they now knew the only point at which we
could land. I contemplated the scene with an anxious ach-
ing heart. The number of troops in the boats was about
5500, and the whole army about 15,000, of which there
were about 1000 sick at the time of landing, and of these

about 400 belonged to our own regiment.—There were
two bomb ketches and three sloops of war, anchored with
their broadsides to the shore: on the right flank of the
boats there were a cutter, two Turkish gun-boats, and two
armed launches; and on the left flank, a cutter, a schooner,
one gun-boat, and two launches. These light vessels were
to go as near the shore as the water would admit, to annoy
the enemy and protect the boats.

At nine o'clock the signal was made for the boats to
advance; and the whole line advanced at the same instant, giving three loud cheers. "The French, to the number of two thousand, were posted on the top of sand-
hills, forming the concave arc of a circle on the front of
about a mile, in the centre of which elevated itself, a
nearly perpendicular height of sixty yards, apparently
inaccessible."* The left of this rising ground was a con-
tinuation of sand-hills close to the shore, gradually
diminishing in their height, until they ended in a long
flat tongue forming the entrance of Lake Maadie. The
ground to the right of the centre height on the shore
was flat, but there were clusters of thick bushes, (such
as form the date or palm tree), which were favourable
for concealing the enemy; and on the extremity of the
right stood the castle of Aboukir, in which were several
10 inch mortars, and a large Martello tower, having two
brass 32 pounders on its top, and which, from its position
and height, commanded nearly the whole shore. As
soon as the boats set off for the beach, the two bomb
ketches, and the three sloops of war, began to throw their
shot and shells upon the shore; and the light vessels,
stationed to protect the flanks of the boats, moved along

* I quote these words from Sir R. Wilson's history, which contains
a degree of knowledge that I could not pretend to. The statements
which I give of the strength of the enemy, the number of cannon they
had on the field on the different days, and what we took from them, I
also state upon his authority. The account of the losses of the army
I take from the statements in the gazettes, which I believe to be pretty
correct, for I have found that they gave a true account of the loss of
my own regiment, and I have heard soldiers of other regiments say
the same of the gazette accounts of the loss of theirs.

G

with them and began to fire. The bulk of the enemy's
field artillery was in the flat ground, to the right of the
height before mentioned, the rest was among the smaller
sand-hills on the left of it. As soon as the boats were
within the reach of their shot, they opened their fire on
them ; and it appeared to be their design, to make their
shot cross the boats in the centre. The heavy guns on
the top of the tower in Aboukir castle, and the mortars,
commenced, at the same time, their fire on the right flank
of the boats. The scene now became dreadful ; the war
vessels pouring whole broadsides; the bomb ketches
throwing shells, which, exploding in the air, formed numerous little clouds ; and the gun-boats and cutters on the
flanks of the boats, exerting themselves to the utmost. As
none of these, however, could approach the shore, so near as
to be within the reach of grape-shot, or even to have a certain aim, their exertions were of little benefit to the boats;
which pursued their progress towards the shore, whilst the
enemy's artillery, (12 pieces, exclusive of the large guns
in Aboukir castle), continued to play upon them with
unremitting activity. All eyes were directed towards
the boats ; every flash of the enemy's artillery was noticed ; and every eye on the stretch, to discern where the
shot might strike the water, to observe if it lighted among
the boats, and if any of them were damaged or sunk ;
and we too often had occasion to picture to our minds,
when we saw the shot strike in the middle of them, and
produce disorder, how many it might have killed, or
wounded, or drowned ; for my own part, although I felt
thankful that I was not myself in the boats, yet my feelings for those that were, were nearly, if not altogether,
as painful, as if I had been in them ; and I believe that
this was the case with the most of the spectators. But
while we were thus feeling for them, we became increasingly astonished to behold how the boats pressed forwards
towards the shore, although the wind, of which there was a
smart breeze, was against them; how well they preserved
their order under the terrible fire of the enemy's artillery;
and how quickly any disorder produced by the shot that
fell amongst them was remedied. The painful feelings of

anxious apprehension and suspense experienced by those in the boats, must have been greatly heightened by the circumstance, that most of the shells and shot fired by our war vessels were necessarily fired over their heads, they being between the vessels and the enemy: so that an ill-directed shot from their own ships, was as dangerous to them as one from the shore; and when buzzing through the air over them, must have been apprehended as one from the enemy, about to strike destruction amongst them.

As the boats approached the shore, the enemy moved their artillery that was on their right, and drew it nearer to their centre. It appeared to be a part of their object, to keep the extreme right of the boats betwixt their artillery and the war vessels, and thus prevent the war vessels from having a clear opening to direct their fire: and indeed all our fire, from all descriptions of vessels, did not seem to interrupt for a moment that of the enemy, or to silence a single gun all the time the troops were rowing to the beach. When they approached near to it, the enemy having drawn their artillery from the right, planted it on the top of the centre height, which now appeared to look directly down upon the boats: and now came the most trying moment. From this elevated position they poured down such a continued fire of shot, shell, and grape, as made us, who were looking on, apprehend that few would reach the shore. Some disorder too appearing among the boats increased our fears; but at this instant we heard them begin to cheer, and saw them press forward with redoubled vigour. We soon observed the right flank of the boats reach the shore under the centre height,* and the men form immediately on the beach; while the enemy from the top of the height poured down grape-shot, as well as the fire of musketry from a line of infantry which was ranged along it. In a few seconds the 40th flank companies, and the 23d regiment, were in line; and, without firing a shot, ascended the height in the face of the enemy. This

* The boats had gradually verged to the left during their progress, so that this height, which before appeared to be opposite their centre, was now opposite their right.

movement was clearly seen by the whole fleet, and attracted all eyes. The spectators began to tremble, lest the enemy should drive them down again; but we were astonished to see with what rapidity and order they mounted the steep face of the height. They were soon close to the enemy, and charged them with loud cheers, when the enemy fled, and in an instant both parties were out of sight. The 42d regiment, which had landed and formed, was now seen ascending the left of the height, and charging the enemy opposed to them, who also fled and disappeared. We now turned our attention more to the left, where part of the troops were forming on the beach; but the left of the boats had not yet reached the shore. The enemy, who had been posted among the smaller sand-hills, as soon as the boats came near the shore, rushed down into the water, fired into them, and endeavoured to prevent their landing. A party of cavalry also charged those who were in the act of landing, which produced a temporary confusion; but they were soon wholly repulsed. All the troops were landed, and the beach, and the heights that lined it, cleared of the enemy, I believe, in less than a quarter of an hour, and nothing to be seen by the spectators, but the empty boats, hoisting their sails, and proceeding with all possible speed to receive the second division. Some of them soon reached the ship I was in, and with all haste we got into them and rowed for the shore. On the way I saw some boats swamped, which had been struck with large shot; but the men who were in them had been picked up by the small boats, which followed those that had troops in them, for this express purpose. The number of boats, that were seriously damaged, was small, compared with what might have been expected; but they were in general less or more perforated with grape shot and musketry. The boat in which I was had an oar broken, and was otherwise damaged; but none of the men were killed or seriously wounded in her.

We soon reached the shore, at a place where it was deeper than common: and with a leap I landed dry shod. The first thing I saw, as I passed along the beach, was some Frenchmen lying dead within the edge of the wa-

ter. The beach was strewed with dead and wounded
men, with horses, and artillery taken from the enemy :
but the action was over. We formed in a hollow on the
left of the centre height, where the 42d had repulsed a
charge of cavalry; some of the 42d, and also of the
cavalry, with their horses, were stretched dead upon the
sand :—we were soon ready, and advanced through the
first range of sand-hills, and found the first division formed with their artillery, which had landed along with them,
and was drawn by seamen. This circumstance had materially contributed to the success of the landing; for
the enemy were astonished to find that our artillery was
landed as soon as the troops, and began to fire upon them
as soon as the musketry of the infantry. Eight pieces
of cannon were taken from the enemy; but the army lost
in this affair, one hundred and two killed, five hundred
and fifteen wounded, and thirty-five missing; the loss of
the navy was twenty-two killed, seventy-two wounded,
and three missing, making a total of seven hundred and
forty-nine, the greater part of which were killed or
wounded in the boats, previous to landing.

During the course of the day, the troops were all
landed; we did not however advance far that day, but
took up a position at no great distance from the shore.
Our first concern was to learn whether water could be
got in this sandy desert; and we were glad to find
that it could be obtained in the hollows, by digging a little way in the sand. When night came on we stationed
our guards, and lay upon the sand, covering ourselves
with our blankets. This night I was surprised to find
that I could see nothing, and I continued to be in this
state every night, until the night of the 20th: in the
day time I saw as well as ever I did, and had no pain in
my eyes.

On the morning of the 9th our regiment, along with
a party of Corsican riflemen, advanced along the peninsula about three miles from where we landed, to a place
where it was contracted into less than half a mile in
breadth. Here was a redoubt and a flag-staff, for communicating signals betwixt Aboukir castle and Alexandria: but the enemy had left it, and thrown a large gun,

intended to be mounted on it, into the ditch. In the course of the day, the 42d regiment and others, came and occupied this position, and we returned to our former one, where we remained until the morning of the 12th, waiting for the landing of some horses, ammunition, and provisions, from the fleet. We made booths of the branches of the date (or palm tree), to shelter ourselves from the dew, which fell very copiously, and we had sometimes heavy showers of rain and hail, which made it pretty cold. The thermometer was frequently below 50.

On the morning of the 12th, having filled our canteens with water, and furnished ourselves with three days provisions, the whole army advanced. Having proceeded a little beyond the narrow neck of the peninsula, the enemy's cavalry began to skirmish; our march was slow and often interrupted; the surface of the ground being very uneven, the sand very deep, and the day very warm, parties were frequently sent to assist the seamen with the guns, and even those guns which had horses to draw them, were unable to get forward, for the horses had never been used to the draught, and were often unmanageable.—Before evening we came within sight of the enemy's army posted on a height. Their strength was about 6000 men, of which 600 were cavalry, with 20 to 30 pieces of cannon. As it was too late to engage them that night, we halted, and began to dig for water; for we had made use of all that we had, and were now very thirsty. The place where we began to dig, was a deep soil of black earth, and below it a clayish mixture. About four or five feet from the surface, water began to appear in small quantities; each company dug a well, but before the one to which I belonged had found water, the regiment was ordered upon picquet. There was no help for it. We were posted along the front of the army, only those who were blind were not put on sentry, but left in groupes, a little in the rear. There were nearly twenty of a company in this condition. We felt very unhappy; for we had to remain in the spot where we were, until, when it was necessary to shift our position, some one who had sight came to conduct us to ano-

4

ther place: we then took hold of one another, and were led in a string ; and, had a party of the enemy made a dash at the place where we were, we were unable either to have resisted or fled.

On the morning of the 13th we were ordered to advance in front of the army, to form, along with the 90th regiment, the advanced guard. We had no time to procure water, but got a little rum, and began our march, leaving our knapsacks with a guard. We had not advanced far, before our light company, which was in front, came upon the enemy's picquets, and a skirmishing began, which increased as we advanced. The light company was reinforced several times, the enemy's picquets getting stronger as they retreated, being joined by those who were in their rear. The ground through which we marched was interspersed with thick bushes; but we approached a rising ground, on which the main body of the enemy's army was drawn up in order of battle. The ascent to this height was entirely bare, and also the ground to the left of it, which projected to Lake Maadie. Our regiment kept to the side of the lake; the 90th was on our right ; and the army followed us in two lines. Our parties in front pressed eagerly upon the enemy's picquets, which caused the regiment to march pretty quickly, in order to be near them for their support ; and this led us to get a considerable way in advance of the army, which could not follow with the same speed. There was one nine pounder field-piece, and one 4½ inch howitzer, along with us ; but very little ammunition with them. Armed launches too had kept pace with the left of the army upon the lake ; but it was now so shallow that they could not follow us farther.—As soon as the 90th regiment had cleared the broken ground, and began to ascend the height on which the enemy's army was posted, a heavy column of cavalry was observed coming forward to charge them. The front section of the 90th halted, and the regiment formed line with all expedition. The front section of the enemy's cavalry wheeled, as soon as it came opposite the right of the 90th, and began to form line. The two parties formed opposite and very near each other, but the cavalry line was formed first. The rear sections of the 90th had not time to reach the extent of the line, and closed upon the rear of the left, making it six or eight deep, but they had a clear view of the horsemen who were on higher ground. The cavalry advanced upon them with their swords raised; the 90th stood firm, until the cavalry were so near the right of their line, that they were going to strike at them with their swords; they then began to fire, and it ran from right to left like a rattling peal of thunder. It was one of the most terrible discharges of musketry I ever saw; and, from the nearness of the enemy, it was dreadfully destructive. The cavalry instantly retreated, and many horses ran away with empty saddles. During the time of this transaction, which was over in a few seconds, our regiment made a momentary pause. On the retreat of the cavalry we again advanced. The enemy then began to open their artillery upon us from the heights. We still pressed on; but as they saw all our movements, and perceived that we were considerably advanced before the army, they formed the resolution to attack us with all their force; and accordingly marched to their right down the height, and, when on the plain, formed line, and came forward. When we perceived their movement, we halted, formed five companies in line, posted the other five in the rear of scattered bushes on the left towards the lake, and awaited their approach. We cannonaded them with our two pieces, but our ammunition being soon expended, the guns were drawn into the rear.

During the time that we were advancing, I had frequently and earnestly prayed to God, to spare and protect me. Our present situation was one of imminent danger; part of the enemy's artillery were playing upon us from the rising ground towards the right; and in front, the enemy, with the rest of his artillery, was advancing in great force, in a line formed like the blade of a scythe, the curved point to our left on the shore of the lake, and that part of it appeared to be composed of cavalry.* It seemed to be the enemy's intention to come round our left, and get into our rear with that part

* It was afterwards said that it was the dromedary corps.

of their line, while the rest of it attacked us in front, and out-flanked us on the right, by which they would have completely surrounded us, and either destroyed or carried us prisoners, before the main body of the army could arrive to assist us. This was their only object. They were too weak to attack the army on level ground with any hope of success; but they were more than competent to take or destroy our party, which did not amount to 500 men. I was near the left of the line, and beheld the advance of the enemy with an anxious mind; but as we were standing in a fixed position, I had some leisure for reflection; and as death was once more staring me in the face, I began to inquire " what hope have I for eternity, if I am cut off at this time?" I confessed my sins in the words of the 51st Psalm; and besought God to pardon them, and give me a new heart; I then thought, " If we are mostly cut down at this time, and have to appear before God, will he make no difference between me and those around me, many of whom, in place of calling upon him, profane his name?" I then endeavoured to lay hold on the mercies promised to the penitent and contrite in heart. I thought I was sorry for my sins, and confessed them without guile, and on this account I endeavoured to hope for mercy, thus resting partly on the difference that I conceived to be between my own character and that of others, and partly on my contrition and repentance before God. But my mind was still dissatisfied; I still feared the worst; I knew not the merits of a Saviour's righteousness; my hope was not built upon him but on myself, and could not be satisfactory. I therefore cried to God to spare me once more, and promised that my future life should be devoted to his service. The Lord was pleased to hear my cry, and to protect me during the awful scene that was just about to commence. The enemy's line had advanced within about 300 yards, and brought two-field pieces in front of the company I was in, and fired them at us. One of the balls came skimming along the surface of the ground. I caught a view of it at some distance, and thought it was coming directly to me. It grazed a small hillock of rubbish a few yards in our front, and laid down the second file on my right. It struck the left leg of the front rank

man in the centre, passing through it, and leaving a part
of the skin on each side. It grazed the calf of the rear rank
man's left leg, tearing it, and carrying part of it away.
The small stones which it drove from the rubbish-hillock
hurt our faces, and a quantity of them entered into the
lacerated limbs of the wounded like hail. The one whose
leg was broken died some time after he had undergone
amputation; the other also died some months after in Rosetta. I thought that the hillock of rubbish had perhaps
altered the direction of the ball, else it might have struck
me; and while I felt for my comrades, I thanked God
that I had escaped.

We were now anxious for orders to commence firing,
as the enemy were still marching forwards; the ground
in front was somewhat undulated, rising a little, for
about 200 yards in our front, and then gently falling.
Our commanding officer allowed them to advance, as far
as to the highest part in our front; and whenever we saw
their feet distinctly, gave orders to fire. This was eagerly done; and the moment we began firing, the enemy's
line, in place of rushing forward, and destroying us in an
instant, made a halt from right to left, and opened their
fire upon us. As we were most afraid of the two pieces
of artillery in front playing upon us with grape-shot,
those around me directed their fire chiefly at them,
which I believe caused them to be removed to one of the
flanks. We then levelled at those directly in our front;
but the smoke soon covered them so much, that a particular object was not visible. We then took aim at
where we judged their line was; but we were not so
much afraid of those directly in our front, as of a body
which appeared to be cavalry, and which threatened to
come round our left into our rear. In order to keep
them back, those near me directed nearly the one half
of their fire against them; for we feared that those who
were posted in the rear of the bushes to our left, would
not be able to prevent them from advancing, the bushes
being widely scattered, so that they might have been easily passed. These men, however, did their duty most admirably. The enemy opened a fire of grape-shot, from several
pieces of artillery, to dislodge them; but they bravely

maintained their post. Our ranks were now getting thinner; our commanding officer, Lieutenant Colonel Erskine, was severely wounded with grape shot in several parts of the body.* The officer commanding the company I was in, was also wounded, and many more.—After we had fired about 12 rounds, whilst I was in the act of loading, I was struck by a musket ball in the left side, near the pit of the stomach, close to the ribs, and was whirled round on my heels by the force of the stroke. I was stunned and felt great pain; and, concluding that I was wounded, I stept into the rear, and grasped the place with my hand. I found the skin was entire; and on shaking myself, the ball dropped at my feet. I then resumed my place in the ranks, and continued to fire until I had expended 22 rounds; when to our great joy, a party of marines, doing duty on shore, arrived on our right, and Dillon's regiment on our left. At the first fire of these troops, the enemy retreated with great precipitation. We pursued them to some distance; and Dillon's regiment coming up with a party of them, charged, and took two pieces of cannon. The enemy was so closely pressed that he divided his forces, and part of them retreated to the left, through a shallow place of the Lake Maadie, the other part retired direct upon Alexandria. Had we had a proper proportion of cavalry, we might have captured all the enemy's artillery, and even have taken Alexandria itself; for we could have reached it before that part of the enemy's force which retreated to the left, as we were nearer it than they.

The army formed in line on the heights which the enemy had occupied in the morning: they cannonaded us, and kept up a fire of sharp-shooters, by which we lost a number of men. A division of the army was detached to the left, to a height near to that of Alexandria; the reserve advanced on the right, and another division in the centre. Our regiment was part of the division sent to the left. The day was warm, and we suffered much from want of water. I have seen a Spanish dollar offered

* He was taken on board one of the ships in the fleet, and had one of his legs amputated, but he died in a few days, and was buried on shore, at Aboukir.

for a draught, and in many instances refused. The gun-powder which unavoidably got into our mouths by biting the ends of our cartridges while loading, tended greatly to augment our thirst.

The enemy had now concentrated his forces on the heights of Alexandria. When he saw our division advancing to the left, he sent a party with two guns to cannonade us, and as we advanced nearer, he opened upon us a heavy fire of shot and shell. Our order of march was in divisions of companies; and, as we drew near the height, a cannon ball struck the ground, close to the right of the division of the company I was in. The ground happened to be soft mould; the ball lodged itself in the mould and we were covered with the dust and small fragments of stones which it raised. It was a great mercy that the ground was not hard in that spot, as it was in the greater part of the adjacent ground; for the ball would in that case have rebounded, and in all probability have laid down the front rank of the division. I felt thankful for deliverance, and continued to pray in my heart to God to spare and protect me.—We formed in close columns upon the height. The bed of a canal, over which was a bridge, lay in the bottom of the hollow that was betwixt us and the enemy's position: the bridge was defended by a party of cavalry and infantry, with two guns. The 44th regiment, being sent in front, charged the enemy with the bayonet, and captured the bridge; and the party which defended it retired into their own lines. During this operation, the columns advanced, and began to descend into the hollow. Our regiment was in the front, the enemy played upon us with his artillery, to which we were now dreadfully exposed; but, after we had descended some way down the height, we were ordered to retire; and, as we retreated under cover of the height, we were partly screened from his fire. After we had remained in this position some time, our regiment was allowed to retire, to the rear of the right of the centre division of the army. This division had been formed in line on the plain, and being wholly unprotected from the enemy's shot, had suffered very severely. They were still in this state; but they had now laid down their arms, and either sat or lay on the ground, by which means they were not so much exposed. We took up our position, and several men from each company were allowed to go in quest of water. I was one of them; and, as no one knew where to find it, we took different routes. After travelling some distance to the rear, I got information where water was to be had; and having made all haste to the spot, I found it, and instantly began to drink; but I thought I should never be satisfied. Never was any thing so precious to me in all my life as this water. After having drank a considerable quantity, I began to fill the canteens (of which I had 10), which I had brought to fetch it to those who remained; but many a drink I took before I had filled them. I then began to feel a little hungry, having eaten nothing from the preceding morning, lest it should increase my thirst. I sat down, and took a piece of biscuit and a bit of pork, and began to eat; but still every mouthful required a little of the water; and I wished to be fully satisfied, before leaving the place, that I might not be under the necessity of drinking any of what I was carrying away. The water was white and muddy, but not thick; it was in a part of what had been the bed of a canal, or had been hollowed out by torrents coming from the heights in the winter season, across the mouth of which a bank had been thrown, which prevented the water from running into the lake, to which it was near. Having satisfied my thirst, I returned with a load of water to my comrades, to whom it was as acceptable as it had been to myself. We remained until near sun-set in the same position; and as the whole army was within reach of the enemy's shot, he continued less or more to cannonade us. When our regiment got on their feet and began to move, they fired at us from two of their heaviest guns. One of the balls rebounded from the ground, nearly killed our Major, and passed through the ranks: those opposite to it saw it, and were so fortunate as to make an opening, through which it passed without touching any one.

By sun-set the army took up its position on the heights from which the enemy had been driven on the morning, with our right to the sea, and our left to the canal that separated Lake Maadie from the bed of Lake Mareotis.

H

—As soon as our position was adjusted, and we had liberty to pile our arms, the cry was for more water; and as I had been sent for it before, and knew where it was to be found, I was sent along with others. It was dusk before we reached the spot, which now presented a confused but interesting scene. The cavalry and artillery horses, which had been all day without water, were now there, and had gone into it with their feet, where they were greedily drinking. This had stirred up the mud, and made the water a perfect puddle; near the edge it was as thick as paste. We had therefore to wade in among the horses to where it was deeper; so that here were men and horses, standing promiscuously knee deep in the water, trying as it were which could drink fastest. By the time I got my canteens filled, it was pretty dark; and, owing to the confusion, as I could not see, I had great difficulty in finding the regiment.

I now lay down on the ground to take some rest. I reflected seriously on the events of the past day, and thanked God for having heard my prayers, and for having spared and protected me. I remembered the promises I had made, and my conscience accused me of having broken them almost as soon as made. Even during the time of the action, when many were falling around me, and my danger was greatest, I had made use of improper expressions: expressions which I was not guilty of using at other times, and which, on such an occasion above all others, I ought to have avoided. This threw me into dejection of spirits, and into a train of very serious reflections for several days; reflections which were deepened by my being led to see more minutely the danger I had escaped. Having occasion to shift my clothes, I observed that the ball which had struck me on the side, had passed through my coat and cut my waistcoat between the second and third button from the bottom; it had then grazed my side, and had been obstructed in its passage outwards by a small volume of poems, containing Pope's Essay on Man, Blair's Grave, and Gray's Elegy, which I had in my side pocket. The corner of the binding next to my side was shattered, and the greater part of the leaves much bruised. I now discerned,

I

that it had been the force with which the ball struck
the book that had wheeled me round. I was impressed with the conviction, that if I had been standing
square to my front, the ball would have lodged in my
left side; and that even in the oblique position in which
I stood, had it been one inch nearer the right, it would
have lodged in the body and proved mortal. There were
few of my comrades that had not their clothes cut in several places; and many had received contusions that
would have proved mortal wounds, if the French had
properly loaded their pieces. It was said that they did
not use the ramrod in loading, which enabled them to
fire with greater rapidity; but the charge being loose in
their pieces, the shot did not fly so true to its direction,
and was in many cases weak; making only a contusion,
in place of perforating the body. This partly accounts
for such a long continued and tremendously superior fire, not being so destructive as might have
been apprehended. The regiment lost 125 killed and
wounded; but our wonder was how so many had
escaped.

The loss sustained by the army, was 156 killed, 1082
wounded; and of seamen and marines there were 29
killed and 55 wounded, making a total of 1322. Four
pieces of cannon and some ammunition were taken from
the enemy.

A great part of the grape shot and cannon balls, that
were fired by the French, were made of a composition of
brass. They had taken the copper-sheeting and bells of a
number of the ships in the harbour, and the unserviceable
brass guns in their possession, and had melted them into
balls, to prevent their ammunition from being exhausted;
because the blockade of Egypt by our ships of war, prevented them from receiving regular supplies from France.
But the grape shot of this description that lodged in the
bodies of the wounded, had the tendency of making the
wounds foul.

I continued to ponder over what had taken place; and
my mind became increasingly uneasy. Conviction of
sin, and a sense of ingratitude to God for his mercies,

drove me almost to despair. I had my Bible with me, but made no use of it: our duty and fatigues left almost no leisure to do so, even had I been so inclined; and the dangerous nature of our present situation agitated the mind, and prevented the composure needful for the investigation of truth. One who previously knew the spiritual import of the Scriptures, might have made some profitable use of a Bible; but our circumstances were quite unfavourable for one like me. I was left to ruminate upon what occurred to my memory. I recollected what Manoah's wife said to her husband, when he was afraid that he should die because he had seen God. "If the Lord were pleased to kill us, he would not have received a burnt-offering and a meat-offering at our hands;" (Judges xiii. 23.) and was led to conclude, that I ought not to give myself over to despair, seeing God had yet spared my life. I had also a general recollection of the following passage of Young's Night Thoughts:—

———————————————— Time destroyed
Is Suicide, where more than blood is spilt.
Time flies, death urges, knells call, heav'n invites,
Hell threatens; all exerts: in effort, all;
More than creation labours!—Labours more?
And is there in creation, what, amidst
This tumult universal, wing'd despatch,
And ardent energy, supinely yawns?—
Man sleeps; and *Man* alone; and *Man* whose fate,
Fate irreversible, entire, extreme,
Endless, hair-hung, breeze-shaken, o'er the gulph
A moment trembles; drops! and *Man* for whom
All else is in alarm! *Man*, the sole cause
Of this surrounding storm! and yet *he* sleeps,
As the storm rock'd to rest—Throw *Years* away?
Throw *Empires*, and be blameless. Moments seize,—
Heaven's on their wing: a moment we may wish
When worlds want wealth to buy. Bid *Day* stand still,
Bid him drive back his car, and re-import
The period past; regive the given hour:
Lorenzo, *more* than miracles we want:
Lorenzo—O for yesterdays to come!

Such is the language of the man *awake;*
His ardour such, for what *oppresses* thee:
And is his ardour vain, Lorenzo? No;
That *more* than miracle the gods indulge;
To-day is *yesterday* return'd; return'd

Full-power'd to cancel, expiate, raise, adorn,
And reinstate us on the Rock of peace.
Let it not share its predecessor's fate ;
Nor, like its elder sisters, die a fool.
Shall it evaporate in fume ? fly off
Fuliginous, and stain us deeper still ?
Shall we be poorer for the plenty pour'd ?
More wretched for the clemencies of heav'n ?

NIGHT SECOND.

While I had a general recollection of this passage on
my mind, there were a number of its particular expressions very frequently in my memory. When I thought
on the past dangers I had come through, and looked at
our present hazardous situation, the words

———— " hair-hung, breeze-shaken, o'er the gulph
" A moment trembles,"————

strongly impressed my mind with a sense of the critical
nature of human life in general, and of such a situation
as I was now in, in particular ; and the words,

———————————————— " and yet he sleeps,
" As the storm rock'd to rest"————

with the folly of being careless and unconcerned, in such
a situation ; and when I thought on the misimprovement
of past time, the words

—————————— " O for yesterdays to come !"

spoke the feelings of my heart :—but the words,

" To-day is yesterday return'd ; return'd
" Full-power'd to cancel, expiate, raise, adorn,
" And reinstate us on the Rock of peace,"

were often in my mind, and contributed, with the words
of Manoah's wife, to give me a partial ease ; they led
me to form a new resolution, of setting out once more,
in attempting to lead a godly life, and keep the divine
commandments. Having formed this resolution, I set
about the performance of it with all due care, and my
mind enjoyed a temporary peace. I was frequent in
prayer, as I hoped that by this means, I should prevent
my mind from wandering. I had taken my present resolution so strongly, that I thought if I did not keep it this

time, I could never hope to keep any resolution afterwards.

We now got our tents on shore, and were busily employed in landing the heavy artillery, and in raising breastworks and redoubts. The fatigues of the army were very great; and as nearly the one half were now affected with the night blindness, they were ordered to take their turn of night duties. A blind and a seeing man were put to work together, to carry two-handed baskets filled with earth to raise the breast-works, the seeing one leading the blind; and as the sentries on the out-posts were double, a blind and a seeing man were also put together: the blind man was company to the other; for, although he could not see, he could hear; and more depended upon that than upon seeing, for the best sight could not see an object at night at any distance. When upon sentry at night, I discovered that when I looked a good while down to the ground, I could discern upon *it* the shadows of persons that were approaching me; but if I lifted up my head, I could not see the persons themselves, though they came close to my face. I continued, when out at night, to look constantly to the ground, and my sight gradually got better, and was quite recovered by the night of the 20th.

During the march of the army from Aboukir, I had seen great quantities of ruins; and while employed in working among them, and in building breast-works and redoubts with the stones of ancient palaces, and the earth that formed the banks of their far-famed canals, I could not but reflect on the ancient glory of Egypt, of which there were so many evidences, even in the barren peninsula of Aboukir. I saw in these ruins the fulfilments of Jehovah's threatenings, and an evidence of the truth of the Scriptures;—and from the description given of " populous No," (Nahum iii. 8, 9, 10. Ezekiel xxx. 14, 15, 16. which I had frequently read during the passage up the Mediterranean,) I conceived that somewhere in this vicinity, such a city must have stood. These reflections gave an unusual degree of interest to our operations. We were now upon Scripture ground: we had come from a distant island of the sea, to the land of the proud Pharaohs, to carry on our military operations, where Nebuchadnezzar, and Alexander the Great, had carried on on theirs. The event was singular and striking: and our situation novel and interesting. Our camp stretched from the sea to the lake; and on the lake were numerous boats, bringing provisions, ammunition, and military stores from the fleet; while parties of seamen and soldiers, were carrying or dragging through the deep sand, the various articles from the landing place, distant about two miles from the position of the army. And within 4 miles of our front, were the heights of Alexandria, upon which the enemy's troops were posted, with the various forts which they had constructed for their defence. On the right of their position stood the beautiful and majestic column, known by the name of "Pompey's Pillar;" and towards their left stood the stately obelisk called "Cleopatra's Needle."* The old walls of

* For the information of such readers as have not access to large works, I will take the liberty of inserting an account of the dimensions of these celebrated and ancient monuments, from Sir R. Wilson's history.

"Pompey's Pillar is of the Corinthian order, and eighty-eight feet six inches in height; the shaft formed of a single block of granite, retaining the finest polish, except where the wind on the north-east front has chafed the surface a little; it is sixty-four feet in height, and eight feet four inches in diameter.

"About thirty yards in the rear of the French intrenchment, stands Cleopatra's Needle, and one of equal magnitude is lying close by, horizontally. The form of these obelisks is of considerable elegance, and their magnitude is enormous, considering that each is only one piece of granite; their height is sixty-eight feet three inches, and their base seven feet seven inches by seven feet square; their sides are covered with hieroglyphics, which, on the eastern front of the one that is upright, are much effaced by the wind.

"Tradition affirms that they ornamented the gate of Cleopatra's palace. From the quantity of marble, &c. &c. found near the spot, probably the residence of the sovereigns of Egypt was placed there."—*History of the Expedition*, 2d vol. pp. 156, 158, 159.

Dr. E. D. Clark, the traveller, who has paid great attention to the study of the age and design of ancient monuments, thinks that the *shaft* of Pompey's Pillar "is of much earlier antiquity than either the *capital* or the *pedestal*." He gives probable reasons to believe that the *shaft* was made in the time of *Alexander the Great*, the founder of *Alexandria*, and who was buried there, to be a sepulchral pillar to the memory of that monarch; but that *Julius Cæsar* had set it upon a *pedestal*, and had put a *capital* upon it in honour of Pompey, whose

Alexandria were behind them, over which the masts of near 200 sail of ships were visible, which had conveyed the army of Buonaparte from France, and had been blockaded by the English since that time. And in the more distant view to the sea, was the Isle of Pharos, at the entrance of the harbour, on which once stood a light-house, mentioned by Rollin in his Ancient History as one of the seven wonders of the world, but which was now strongly fortified by the French, for the protection of the harbour, before which a squadron of our fleet kept constantly cruizing.

The Arabs began to bring us sheep and young onions for sale. The men of the tent I was in, bought a sheep for a Spanish dollar, from an Arab, whose only covering was a plaid thrown round his naked body, resembling those worn by Highland shepherds. But our greatest difficulty was to find wood to cook it with. The bark of the date tree was the only part of it that would burn: its withered leaves, with the roots of a creeping kind of brier, which we pulled out of the sandy soil, and with difficulty got to burn, were the only fuel we could find. For a few days we had far to travel for water; but every regiment dug wells in the flat ground on the left of the position, where a sufficient supply, although somewhat brackish, was obtained.

My mind continued pretty easy for three or four days; but I found that I was not fulfilling the task that I had undertaken; that I was failing in the performance of duty, and was not keeping God and eternity in view, in the manner I had resolved to do. This began to make me again uneasy; and, as my hopes rested on my own performances, when I found that these performances were not what I had promised and resolved they should be, these hopes were shaken. I had not, indeed, been guilty of any open and notorious sins; but I had not done that which I had resolved to do, and on the doing of which I had hoped for the forgiveness of past

head he caused to be burnt with funeral honours, and the ashes put into an *urn*, and placed on the top of the *pillar*: but that the *pillar* had likely fallen afterwards, and had been restored by the emperor *Hadrian.*—*Clarke's Travels*, 4th *Edit.* 8vo. vol. v. ch. vii. p. 361, &c.

sins, the favour of God, and eternal life; and this threw me back where I was before.

The regiment received orders on the 20th, to march early next morning to Aboukir, to do the hospital duty, because we were too weak to do the duty of a regiment in the line. We were accordingly under arms and marched off an hour before day-light, and left our tents standing for a regiment that was to come from the second line to occupy our place. But we had not proceeded above a mile and a half, when we heard a discharge of several muskets on the left; which caused us to halt and look to the place where the firing had been. In a few seconds, we saw a number more muskets fired, (for the darkness made the flash of even the pan of every musket distinctly visible), and after that a field-piece, and then a general discharge of about 300 muskets; when it ceased. We knew that there was a guard of about 300 men, and a field-piece, with a working party of as many more, on the spot; and as the firing had ceased, we thought it might be a false attack to disturb the working party and alarm the army.—After standing a little, and all continuing quiet, we began with hesitation to proceed on our journey: but we had not moved many steps, when we heard the discharge of a musket on the right of the army : this produced a voluntary halt ; and in a few seconds we heard the discharge of two or three more. We were then ordered to return, and had not proceeded far, before a number more discharges were heard in the same direction. This quickened our march, and we made all expedition towards the tent of the commander-in-chief, which was in the rear of the right of the army. Before we got there, the firing on the right was beginning to be pretty thick. We were now ordered to resume the position we had left. It was yet dark; but the firing of musketry began to be heavy, and the artillery commenced playing, with the help of lighted lanterns to let them see to load. By the time we got to our position, the action was close and warm on the right, and the firing of musketry and artillery very heavy, which the darkness of the morning made peculiarly awful. There was now no doubt of a powerful and determined attack from the enemy. When we arrived at our position in the line, the day had begun faintly to dawn. The regiment which was to have taken our place, had not done it; a column of the enemy having ascended the brow of the hill in our front, were making towards the opening in the line where we should have been. The regiment on the right was extending its left, and the one on the left its right, and had filled up the one half of the space when we arrived. On our arrival a part of us filled up the opening, and began to fire on the enemy's column, which then retreated under the brow of the hill, out of our sight and below the range of shot. They left, however, a number of sharp-shooters on the edge of the hill, who kept up a straggling fire upon our line. The regiments on the right and left now closed their files, and we got all into line and in good order; when the enemy's column, having adjusted itself under the brow of the hill, showed itself anew, and came forward to the attack. We again opened our fire upon them, which they returned; but after the second or third round, they again retreated as before, leaving a still greater number of sharp-shooters, who ranged themselves along the edge of the descent of the hill, which in part concealed them from us, but allowed them to have a fair view of our line, upon which they kept up a destructive fire. We returned a straggling fire upon them from the line, having no sharp-shooters in front to engage them.

When on the way back to the army, previously to entering upon this action, the state of my mind was rather different from what it had been before. I prayed earnestly for protection: but having so often failed in the promises I had made, I was afraid to make any more. I began to be diffident of myself. I did not plead with God on the promise of future amendment, but prayed for mercy. I used indeed the name of Christ; but had no right understanding, either of the true nature of the atonement for the guilt of sin, by his blood, or of his righteousness to justify the ungodly. My confidence was not placed in them for acceptance with God; but should death be the issue, I cast myself, with trembling hesitation, on his general mercy, and that with more resignation than formerly. I confessed my past failures, and prayed that if God was not pleased to preserve me unhurt, but if I was to be wounded, it might be in a merciful way; and that, if death was to be the issue, my sins might be pardoned. This was my prayer on entering the action, and as we had intervals of firing, I repeated it. But great as my fear of death was, I never thought of attempting to avoid it, by flinching from my duty as a soldier in such times of danger. I looked upon such conduct as sinful, and dared not seek present safety, by an increase of guilt. I was also convinced, that cowardice was attended with the greatest danger, and that our greatest safety lay in every one doing his duty with steady courage. I had fired about twelve rounds, when the sun was beginning to appear in the horizon, and was in the act of ramming another cartridge, when a shot from one of the sharp-shooters, struck upon the inner ancle bone of my left foot; it turned round the back of the leg, passing between the sinew of the heel and the leg bone, and lodged just under the skin, a little above the bone of the outer ancle. It was there that I felt the pain. I was stunned with the stroke; but from the part in which I felt the pain, I did not think it was a ball, but that a large shot or shell, having struck some of the stones that were lying in the rear, a splinter from them had hit me in the back of the leg: I loaded my piece, and then, on lifting up my leg to see what was the matter, saw a musket-shot hole in the half-gaiter and some appearance of blood. I shouldered my piece, but the sharp-shooters directly in front of me had disappeared. I stood a few seconds unresolved what to do; but feeling the pain increase, and seeing the blood beginning to appear more on the gaiter, and the officer commanding the company having come to the rear, and observing that I was wounded, he called to me to fall out, and I was induced to leave the ranks, but felt very reluctant to quit my comrades before the battle was decided: not that I loved to stay in a place of danger; but I did not like to leave them in the time of it; and had there been firing at the time, I should have continued to fire while

I was able. As matters stood, however, I conceived it to be my duty, seeing I was disabled from keeping my place in the ranks, to make the best of my way, as long as I was able, to a place where I might be out of the reach of shot, and get my wound dressed, that it might not receive injury by delay. I got as quickly as I could to the rear, keeping my arms, accoutrements, and knapsack which I had on when wounded. The battle at this time was raging upon the right with terrible fury; and the brigade of guards immediately on the right of ours, were closely engaged. The roar of the artillery was dreadful. Day-light had now made both parties visible to each other; but the smoke of the firing obscured the distant view; so that, although the scene of contest was but a short way off from me, I could neither see our own line nor that of the enemy, all being covered with a thick cloud, through which nothing was visible, but the dark red glare of the flashes of the artillery. As I began to descend the height in the rear of the army, I was in imminent danger. The position of the brigade of guards, (which was on the right of ours), and of the right of our own brigade, receded considerably from the spot on which our regiment stood, owing to the direction of the rising ground on which we were posted. In consequence of this and of the positions of the enemy's columns and artillery, a large proportion of his shot, that had been fired at too high an elevation, fell in the rear of our regiment's tents. As I did not at the time observe this circumstance, I took the direct road from our own rear, to the landing place on Lake Maadie, distant about two miles. I was led by this route to cross the range of the falling shot. The musket and grape shot was coming down in showers, and further on, the large shot was striking and rebounding off the ground in rapid succession. I used all possible exertion to get through this danger; and, by the goodness of God, received no further hurt; while others, who, like myself, were wounded and retiring to the rear, did not escape. The exertion I had made, with the blood I was losing, which marked my steps in the sand, began to exhaust me; but I had the happiness of having my canteen full of water at the commencement of my retreat, which refreshed me. My arms, at length, however, becoming too heavy for me, I left my firelock in an erect posture, by running the bayonet into the ground, after taking the powder out of the pan, to prevent accidents to those that might find it.

When I had got near to the landing place, I found several surgeons, on the outside of an hospital tent that had been lately pitched for the sick, busily engaged in dressing some of the wounded that had arrived before me. I sat down to wait my turn to be dressed, which was not long, for the number before me was not great. When I took the gaiter off my leg, I pulled a piece of it out of the wound, and as the ball appeared prominent under the skin, it was easily extracted, and another piece of the gaiter was taken out, which was wrapped round it. The ball was flattened, and a part of it turned over by the resistance of the ancle bone; yet the bone was not broken. After I was dressed, I lay down at the side of a bush, until I might learn what was to be done with the wounded. By this time the firing of musketry had ceased on the field of battle ; a cannonade alone was heard ; and we were all anxiety respecting the success of the day, for if the army was compelled to retreat, the situation of the wounded would be distressing and dangerous. Great numbers of wounded were now arriving to be dressed, who brought different reports, some of them saying, they did not think that the army would be able to keep its ground. This made us look with anxiety to the heights, to observe, if any retrograde motion was made ; but the cannonade ceased ; and we were informed that the enemy had been completely repulsed, and had retreated back to Alexandria. The action terminated about ten o'clock, *a. m.*

This action, though short, was severe and bloody, and was sustained on our part chiefly by the right wing of the army, the left having been only partially engaged. The object of the enemy was to dislodge the troops on the right, from the rising ground on which they were posted, and then to drive the army into Lake Maadie. He expected to possess himself of the rising ground before day break ; and being perfectly acquainted with the place,

I

and with the way in which we were posted, he was at no
loss to make his attack in the dark: but as it was our
practice to stand under arms from three o'clock in the
morning, till an hour after day-break, we were not taken
by surprise. The enemy's force consisted of nine thousand seven hundred men, of which fifteen hundred were
cavalry; with forty-six pieces of cannon. Our army, by
its losses in the former actions, by parties absent at Aboukir on duty, and by sickness, had been reduced to somewhat less than ten thousand, including four hundred cavalry; with thirty-six pieces of cannon. When the enemy retreated, he left seventeen hundred men dead and
wounded on the field, of whom a thousand and forty were
buried the first two days: he lost also four hundred horses. How many wounded retired, or had been removed,
could not be known; but military judges calculate the
whole at about four thousand men, which was more than
a third of their whole number. We had two hundred
and forty-three killed, one thousand one hundred and
ninety-three wounded, and thirty-two missing, and four
seamen killed, and twenty wounded, making a total of
1493.—Our worthy Commander-in-chief, Sir Ralph Abercrombie, died on the 28th, of a wound he received in the
thigh, and was deeply regretted by the whole army. General Moore also was again wounded, but recovered in a
short time and returned to his duty. The loss of our regiment was forty men.

Having lain at the bush until about two o'clock, I then
observed a number of the wounded going on board of
boats to be taken to the fleet. I got up and went to the
landing place, and having got on board one of them, arrived at the fleet in the evening; where I was put on
board a two decked ship appropriated for the reception of
the wounded, and got into a birth with two more of the
same regiment. Upwards of two hundred wounded men
were collected on board of this ship; and the wounds of
many of them being severe, numbers died during the
first ten days. If any one wishes to know what were the
topics of conversation among so many men in such circumstances, it pains me to state, that our conversation
was about any thing but that one thing which most con-

cerned us, and which ought to have engrossed our whole
attention. About that world to which so many of us
were daily departing, and about that God before whom
so many were so soon to make their appearance, there
was not a word to be heard, except it was in taking his
name in vain. The groans of the dying were to be heard
in various quarters of the ship, but no one, either asking
or telling how a sinner could be saved. Nor was I better than others. I did not improve my mercies. I had
been wounded in a comparatively merciful manner, but
I forgot the God to whom I had made my supplication,
and neglected my Bible. I conversed with one of my
comrades, who was a Scotch Episcopalian, upon church
government, and he took some pains to inform me of the
claims of Episcopacy, of which I was ignorant. But what
did such topics avail to dying men, whose conversation
ought to have been about the salvation of their souls?
He was badly wounded in the thigh, and did not live many weeks. The part of my wound where the ball entered, healed in about sixteen days; but the part where it
was extracted became inflamed, and the foot and ancle
swelled considerably. I was suspicious that the dirty
water with which it was sometimes washed was the occasion of the inflammation. An erroneous opinion was entertained, that salt water would smart the wounds: and
as fresh water was not in plenty on board the ship, only
a small quantity of it was allowed for washing them. A
great number were washed with one basin-full, and, as
many of the wounds were foul, this was calculated to infect those that were clean. Had salt water been used, a
basin of clean water might have been taken to every one.
I was washed with salt water when in the hospital at A-
boukir, and felt no difference between it and fresh.—By
the end of three weeks, my wound began to mortify. I
was then put into a boat to be taken to the hospital at
Aboukir, along with a number more whose cases were
considered bad. Two were so weak that they were unable to sit, and were laid upon gratings in the bottom of
the boat: one of them died before we reached the shore,
and the other died upon the beach. These cases made
little impression upon my mind; death was becoming fa-

miliar to me, and I looked at it with a careless indifference. When the boat reached the shore I was carried to the Hutts hospital ; which was a building upon a height, erected by the French to serve as barracks to their troops stationed at Aboukir.

It was formed of the trunks of date trees split down the middle; the ends were sunk into the ground; the flat side of one tree, was turned outwards, and the flat side of the next inwards, and so alternately, the round edges being made to overlap each other, and the crevices filled with plaister lime. It was roofed in the same manner. A great many bats had formed their nests in the holes, where the roof rested upon the upright posts.—Here I was well taken care of; so that by the mercy of God, the inflammation subsided, and in sixteen days the putrid flesh was wholly cleaned away, leaving a pretty large orifice. A part of the tendon of the heel seemed to have been eaten away by the inflammation, but the damage did not appear to be very serious, and it began to heal rapidly.

While in this place, a small scorpion had got into my haversack, and as I put my hand into it to get some bread, it stung me in the point of my thumb. This sensation resembled that which is produced by the sting of a bee, but the pain was more violent, and lasted for twenty-four hours before it subsided, but was attended by no other bad consequence.

The regiment to which I belonged, being at this time encamped at Aboukir, made an offer to accommodate their own wounded men, as the general hospital was crowded. This offer was accepted, and those that were in a condition to be moved were sent to the regimental hospital. I remained a day or two there ; but, being healthy and my wound likely to heal soon, I was removed to the convalescent tents, which, on account of some cases of fever in the regimental hospital, were at some distance. There I was left to dress my wound myself, which continued to mend, but not so rapidly as before. That dreadful calamity, the plague, made its first appearance at the Hutts hospital, about the time that I left it; and, a few days afterwards, a corporal went with a party and buried a surgeon and two women in one hole, and seven others in another, that had already fallen victims to it.

The strength that the enemy brought to the field on the 21st March, showed that they were far more numerous in Egypt than we had been led to believe. The greatest number that had been calculated to be there was 15,000; but they had 27,000. As soon as the action of the 21st was over, the army made trenches along the whole position, and completed and increased the batteries and redoubts with all possible haste. The left was the weakest part of the position. The bed of Lake Mareotis was in front of it, but it was nearly dry, and passable in many parts both for horse and foot. Lake Maadie * was in the rear of the left, being only separated from the bed of Lake Mareotis by the banks of the canal † of Alexandria; and its waters were considerably above the level of Lake Mareotis and the surrounding country. On the 13th April a large opening was made in the banks of the canal; the water rushed into Lake Mareotis with a fall of six feet, and it continued to rush in for a month, when it nearly found its level; but there continued always a fall of about a foot, owing to the sand absorbing the water. By this measure a large extent of country was inundated; the front of the position was contracted, and the left protected from assault; and Lord Hutchison, who had succeeded Sir Ralph Abercrombie, was enabled to proceed with a part of the army to Rosetta, which had been previously taken by a detachment, assisted by 4,000 Turks; General Coote being left with the

* Or Sed; "sometimes called the Lake of Aboukir. The passage into it at Aboukir, is about two hundred yards wide, and was made about the year 1782, by the sea breaking down the dyke, which had been built ages back, to recover from the ocean that part of the country which now is Lake Maadie." *History of the Expedition to Egypt*, p. 27.

† This canal commences at Rhamanieh, on the banks of the Nile, and passes over fifteen or sixteen leagues of country. The bed of it is above the level of Egypt; the banks are formed of earth raised wholly above the surface. There is no water in it, but at the time of the inundation of the Nile. The beds of the canals in Egypt are all above the level of the country, that, when cut, the water may run out of them. They are properly canals of irrigation.

remainder to blockade Alexandria. The force assembling at Rosetta was destined to march against Grand Cairo. The Grand Vizier was advancing with an army from Syria to co-operate in the same object. Our regiment was ordered to join the troops at Rosetta. Most of the men belonging to it, who had been left on board ship sick of the fever, at the time we landed, had by this time recovered, so that it was now pretty strong. I continued in the convalescent tents about a fortnight. To enable me, when necessary, to go abroad, I procured a rough piece of wood, upon which I got the head of a tent mallet fastened, to serve for a crutch. By the help of this, and of a stick in the other hand, I made a shift to go out of the tent; but, not being very expert at the use of the crutch, as I was going out one day, the tent cords catched the lower end of it, and I fell down, with the wounded leg undermost. This was to me a serious accident; for my wound immediately began to get worse, and in a few days it was greatly inflamed and discharging black matter. I was then removed to the hospital tents, to be near the surgeon. Orders came for the regimental hospital to be moved to Rosetta, and such cases as were not fit to be moved were sent to the general hospital, which was now an extensive establishment; for the sick and wounded that were on board the fleet were sent on shore, and lodged in large sheds. Into one of these I was taken, along with another, who had been in the same convalescent tent with me. He had been slightly wounded: a musket ball having grazed the front of his leg; he was able to walk about with little inconvenience, and was desired by the surgeon not to confine himself close to the tent, but to take the air, and some little exercise. We were not, however, aware of the extreme danger of having the skin broken in Egypt, let the hurt be ever so slight. His wound had got much worse; it was not to appearance so serious as mine, yet, after he was a few days in the general hospital, it was found necessary to amputate his leg, an operation which he did not survive long; for the stump mortified, and he died, after lingering about five weeks. His case alarmed me not a little; and as my wound continued for sometime to get worse, the inflammation spreading, the lower part of the leg swelling greatly, and the pain being excessive, I was the more apprehensive, and prayed earnestly for mercy. God was pleased to hear my cry, and to spare me once more. The inflammation by and by subsided; the pain became moderate, my appetite, which was lost, returned; and the wound began to clean and heal.

The weather was now very warm. The shed in which I was, was so constructed, as to combine the advantages of shade and air. The roof was formed of boards, (brought I suppose from Marmorice,) and was supported upon posts, made of the trunks of date trees, which were sunk into the ground at certain distances; boards were nailed to these posts, and about an inch left open betwixt each board to the height of about four feet; and then there was an opening of about two feet to the edge of the roof. This shed was of great length, and was crossed by one or two similar ones. In them all, there were three rows of beds, two rows with the ends of the beds to the sides of the shed, and one row set length-ways in the centre. Although these structures were so open in the sides we were sufficiently warm during the night. We were, however, much troubled with fleas, of which the sandy floor was full, so that it was impossible to get rid of them. Indeed the whole of the desert was full of these vermin. There were also some crickets of a very large size, which interrupted our sleep, by the strong and constant sound of their music; not unmelodious in itself, had it not been unseasonable. The flies too gave us a vast deal of annoyance through the day. It was with difficulty that we could keep them out of our eyes; and they were most pernicious to those who had large putrid sores; for, as it was impossible to keep them out of the wound while it was dressing, this occasioned not only present trouble, but the breeding of maggots, which increased the torture of many, who were sinking to the grave. Even those who were well, of all classes, found it needful to carry a small bunch of rushes tied upon a handle, to be used like a fan, to drive them away.

On the 23d of May, the hot wind came on. The air was darkened with mist, which was so thick that it ren-

dered breathing difficult. We were glad to cover ourselves over the head with our blankets : for although the
heat was intense, and the blankets disagreeably warm and
heavy, yet we found our breathing more tolerable under
them, than when uncovered. The orderly men, who
had to go out of the shed for water, and on other necessary business, complained of the heat of the wind, saying that it blew the sand in their faces as hot as fire.*
Towards evening the wind blew from the sea; the air
became clear; and the night was about its usual coolness.
But the consequences of this wind, were dreadful to the
hospital. The plague now raged with redoubled fury,
and made fearful havock among the nurses and orderly
men, and those who had slight wounds. The three nurses who attended the division of the shed I was in, were
infected one after the other, and were sent to the pest
hospital ; where, as I afterwards heard, they died. One
set of nurses and orderly men followed another in rapid
succession for some weeks. It was observed, that none

* This wind was still more dreadful in the interior of the country,
and at the place where the army was on its march to Cairo ; as appears
by the following extract from Sir R. Wilson's History of the Expedition to Egypt, vol. I. p. 177.

"ALGUM, 23d May.

" This day will ever be remarkable to the Egyptian army ; a
sirocco wind darkened with a burning mist the atmosphere; the thermometer was at 120 in the shade; the ground was heated like the floor of
a furnace; every thing that was metallic, such as arms, buttons, knives,
&c. became burning hot ; the poultry, exposed to the air, and several
horses and camels died ; respiration was difficult, and the lungs were
parched with fiery particles. Had the heat continued forty-eight hours,
the effect would have been dreadful : but happily as night drew on,
the wind cooled, and at last changed to the north-west.

" At Balbeis, the thermometer was at 130 ; on the western side of
the Nile 120 ; at Alexandria 105."

Extract from a Journal written by one of my comrades.

" We had one day's hot wind from the south ; it began to blow
about 9 o'clock ; and woe be to him that is far from shelter, as neither
man nor beast can survive in it three days ! It came from the desert
as hot as the opening of an oven door, bringing small sand like mist
along with it. All the sentinels were called in, and the cattle crept
close to the ground and groaned for fear. The buffaloes took to the
river, covering themselves, all but the nose, in the water ; and no man
was able to stir out of his tent until the evening.

of those who had large sores were infected by it; but such sores after this period were more mortal, for mortifications now became rapid in their progress, and baffled the power of medicine to arrest them. Amputations were multiplied, but were mostly unavailing; and even sores comparatively slight, mortified and proved fatal. Some of the cases struck me forcibly.—A sailor who had a slight wound in one of his legs, and who could move about, and be serviceable to those that were bed-fast, went one night to the shore, which was not far off, to get some drink; his leg immediately got worse; in a few days the entire calf of it was one putrid ulcer, with numbers of maggots; poultices, spirits of wine, and other strong liquors, and tinctures were profusely used, but in vain—he died in about a week. Another, whose wound was cured, and who was ordered to join his regiment, absented himself on the night previous to the day appointed for his departure, and that of some others. In a day or two after the party was gone, he appeared in his place with a sore leg. It was believed that he had purposely scratched his shin with a stone; but whatever way he had taken to make it sore, the Surgeon, who had not noticed his conduct, saw that it required dressing, which was done without any particular inquiry; and as none that knew his conduct, liked spontaneously to inform upon him, he was not called in question. It was manifest, however, that cowardice was the cause of his injuring his leg, that he might remain in the hospital until danger was over. But the very means he took to avoid danger, to which he might never have been exposed, proved his destruction. In three or four days, his leg became so much inflamed, that amputation was rendered necessary. This was performed above the knee, but the inflammation had reached the thigh. As he lay nearly opposite to me, I saw the face of the stump when it was dressed. The skin never united; at the second or third dressing, the flesh of the thigh was detached from the bone; so much so, that there was a large cavity underneath the bone, which made it visible almost to the joint. He died before next day, being about ten or twelve days from the time he appeared with his leg sore.—At my left hand lay a

young man, a sailor belonging to the Northumberland,
74, with a large ulcer in the under side of his right arm,
a little below the arm pit. I formed an attachment to
this young man; took a note of his own and his mother's
name, and place of residence, and of the time when his
wages became due; and promised, if I got safe to England, to inform them of these particulars, and of the time
and circumstances of his death, for he was sensible that
death was near. But there is one thing, that gives me
no small pain, when I reflect upon it, to this day; that,
although I saw he was dying, I was not able, with all
the religion I thought I had, to point my dying comrade
to the Saviour. Not having found a Saviour to my own
soul, whatever I might say about religion or religious
subjects, a Saviour, properly so called, was no part of my
system. I who never beheld Jesus, as the Lamb of God
which taketh away the sin of the world, could not point
him out, in that soul-reviving character, to others; neither did there appear to be in this house of death, any
one that could point his dying comrades to a Saviour,
nor any among the dying throng, that were asking after
a Saviour. Whatever emotions might be passing through
the minds of any, the question as to what became of the
soul after death, the hope of heaven, or the fear of hell,
the way to attain the one and escape the other, never became a subject of conversation; and yet if ever circumstances, (short of those of criminals condemned to die,
without any hope of mercy, upon a particular day,) could
have forced such conversation upon a company of sinful
mortals, it must have been the circumstances we were in.
But every one seemed to indulge the hope of life, until
the cold hand of death was already on his heart, and left
him little time to think of that world to which he was
going, and less ability to communicate his thoughts to
others, or to ask, or to receive information. And this
was the case, not in this hospital only, but in all the hospitals I was in, both before and afterwards. I did indeed
say a few words to my dying comrade, about praying for
mercy to his soul, and made use of the name of Jesus in
a formal way; and he continued for several days before
his death, to pray very earnestly to God for mercy, and

made use of that name: but whether he understood the character of Jesus, as a Saviour, and was led to place his dependence upon his merits, is more than I can tell. It may be, that the Spirit of Christ, in his sovereign grace, gave him a saving knowledge of that name that was used at first in ignorance, and led him to trust in him for salvation; but if this was the case, it was known only to himself: he was unable to make it known to others; and, although he had been able to tell me if asked, I was unable to discern it: for he that has not been enlightened by the Spirit of Christ himself, and brought out of darkness into marvellous light, is ill qualified to discern when that change takes place upon others.*

CHAPTER VI.

PREPARATIONS having been made for erecting a general Hospital in the Town of Rosetta, all that were capable of being removed from Aboukir were sent there. I left Aboukir, and was taken on board of a Germ on the 23d June; which sailed in the afternoon; and at day-break next morning, we were near the entrance of the Rosetta branch of the Nile. The surf on the bar, at the mouth of the river, was high; but the Arabs, who navigated the vessel, risked the passage. The hazard on such occasions is considerable, owing to the surf, and the shallowness of the water on the bar: for the vessel is in danger of striking on the bottom between the surges; and, when this takes place, the next wave that comes, is apt either to break over her and fill her with water, or to overset her.—When we came opposite that part of the bar, which the Arabs thought deepest, they pointed the bow of the vessel to it, and clued up the sails that she might have little pitch,

* The promise that I made of informing his relatives, of the time and circumstances of his death, I fulfilled when I came to Ireland, for which I received a letter of thanks from his brother.

and might float as level as possible ; they then got out
hand poles ; and, as soon as she began to lose head-way,
they set the poles to the bottom, and pushed her forward
with all their power, making a great noise, until we got
over the bar into smooth water.   There were several
masts of vessels visible near where we passed, that had
recently been swamped in this dangerous passage. Many
British seamen lost their lives here, for they were ignorant of its real danger, and would hardly be convinced
of it, because it had not at a distance a very dangerous
appearance.   It was not until they had actually got upon
the bar, that the extent and nature of the danger were
perceivable ; and then, to attempt to return against the
wind and surge, is vain ; they must push through, or perish.   At the first I wondered why the Arabs were making so much noise ; but when we came upon the bar my
surprise ceased.   I had never seen any thing like it ; yet
the wind was not stormy, and if such was the state of
this place with a moderate wind, how terrible must it be
in a storm.——As soon as we were in smooth water, the
large sails were again spread out to the wind, we passed
rapidly up the Nile, and in a short time were at Rosetta.

I was soon taken into a large square building, having
a square court in the centre, and piazzas round about from
the bottom to the top ; the ground flat, which was high
in the roof, was occupied as cellars, store-houses, &c.
There were two flats above, the various apartments of
which communicated with piazza'd passages, round the
centre square.   This building, from the largeness of its
size, and the number of its apartments, accommodated a
great many patients, consisting of men of all the different
regiments, promiscuously lodged together.

In coming into a place of this kind, among so many
strange faces, and various and opposite characters, it is a
matter of some consequence, to meet with some one previously known, to whom you can talk, in whom you can
place confidence, and who will act the part of a comrade.
In this respect I was fortunate ; falling in with a man of
my own company, whose bed was next to mine : a young
man of agreeable dispositions.   He was the rear rank
man of the second file from my right, in the battle of the

13th March, who got the calf of his leg grazed by the cannon ball, as formerly related. His leg was now in a hopeful way; and being able to move about with the help of a stick, he was serviceable to me who was confined to bed. In this building we were more cool than on the sands of Aboukir; the flies were not so excessively troublesome through the day; and, as the floor, which was upon arches, was paved with flat stones or large bricks, the fleas were not so numerous. But a new enemy attacked us during the night, which we had not met with before—the musquitoes. They were very troublesome; and there was no way of securing ourselves from their bite, which was very sharp, and for a while had an inflammatory effect; so much so, that every one for some time after his arrival, resembled a person in the height of the measles. Our accommodation and attendance were much better here in many respects. We were provided with sheets for our beds which was very agreeable; for a sheet was as much as one could bear for a covering during the night; nor was even that needed so much for heat, as to be a partial defence against the musquitoes. Our woollen blankets, which would have been quite uncomfortable from their heat, were very useful now to put under us; for our beds being made of branches of the date tree, put across each other, with a slender matt, made of a particular kind of rushes, laid over them to cover the holes, the cross spars soon became prominent, and were very uneasy to lie upon. My knapsack was my pillow, and my blanket, folded *four-ply*, I put under me. Without it indeed, it would not have been possible to lie in the beds; and even with it, they were very uncomfortable, especially for those who were long and close confined to them.

I had not been in Rosetta above a fortnight, when my wound again inflamed and mortified in a most alarming degree; the leg swelled excessively, and the wound became large and jet black, with a most offensive smell. I was very much alarmed; I beheld many dying, whose wounds were in a similar state, and some of them apparently not so bad; the severity of pain deprived me of appetite: nor could I so much as drink the wine that was allowed me. The pain continued to increase; the dis-

K

charge from the wound was great ; I was reduced to a
skeleton, and my strength was failing fast ; I was at the
gates of death ; and, with eternity before me, I was destitute of that discernment of the merits and grace of the
Great Redeemer, which alone can form a sure ground of
confidence, and a true source of consolation to a poor
sinner, ready to perish. I again reflected on my past
life, and accused myself of want of firmness in my resolutions. I thought God had now afflicted me in order to
make me hate sin, and love righteousness ; and that were
I again restored to health, and free from pain, nothing in
this world would be able to make me leave my duty :
and I flattered myself that what I had now suffered had
destroyed the love of sin in my heart. Under this persuasion, being in agony through the severity of pain, I
exclaimed, " Lord, let it suffice thee, for it is enough ;
take but thine hand from me this once !" Although this
was not a prayer becoming a sinner ready to perish, which
ought to have been a supplication for mercy for the sake
of Christ ; yet God was pleased in his compassion to
grant me the thing I sought. He did remove his hand,
and spare my life ; the mortification, after having raged
about three weeks, subsided ; the putrid flesh began to
fall away ; the burning pain left the wound ; and in about
ten days it was clean ; but the mortification had detached, and wholly destroyed, the greater part of the tendon
of the heel. I now looked upon myself as one that had
been rescued from the grave, and the occurrences that
took place immediately, tended still more strongly to im-
press this upon my mind. The wound of my comrade, who
had been serviceable to me when I was so ill, as I began
to mend grew worse ; inflamed ; and in a few days, nearly the whole of the calf of his leg was one putrid mass.
A blood-vessel burst in it during the night ; but he was
in such pain, that he was not sensible of the bleeding,
which continued until day-break, when the floor under
and around his bed was covered with blood. The surgeon was sent for, to whom he said, " I believe Sir, I
have been bleeding to death in the night time, and was
not sensible of it." The bleeding had now ceased, but
he was so weak that he was unable to speak ; and he died

1

in a few hours, and was carried out and buried. The Saviour's words, " One shall be taken and the other left," struck me forcibly in these circumstances : when my comrade, who was so shortly before in a fairer way of recovery than I was, was thus cut off, and I was left as a monument of God's sparing mercy.

His bed was not long empty. In a few days an Irish Grenadier was brought to it, whose case was truly hopeless. He had had a boil on the lower part of the breast, which had mortified ; the mortification had spread over the breast, and had eaten a hole larger than a dollar into the chest, so that when the dressing was off, the inside of the chest was visible. He lived in great agony for about six days, and died ; by which time the hole into the chest was much larger.—In a few days after, the same bed was filled by an artilleryman, a townsman of my own, who had got the calf of one of his legs accidentally bruised. The leg inflamed ; amputation was resorted to ; but, with all the attention the surgeons paid to him, he also died in a very short time. My wound continued to mend ; and as soon as I was able to move, I got a crutch and a staff, and a strap to support my leg, and got out of bed for a part of the day, after having been confined to it nearly six months.

This was about the middle of September, before the Nile had attained the height of its inundation. I passed a part of the day, sitting in one of the front windows which looked to the Nile, and remarked its daily progress. As I grew stronger, I got upon the roof of the building which was flat, and had a view of the town and the surrounding country. In the country, on the opposite side of the Nile, nothing was to be seen, as far as the eye could reach, but water, with the trees standing in it. I travelled about too, visiting my acquaintances in the hospital who belonged to the same regiment with myself.

Some of the Arab watermen were employed to supply the hospital with water. They brought it from the Nile*

* During the time of the inundation, the water in the river is very thick ; but as much pure water as served us for drinking, was procured from some private wells in the town, which I suppose had a communication with the river, which had the effect of filtering the water.

upon their backs, in the skins of goats slung across their shoulders. The skin had been sewed up after being taken off the animal, and was in its natural shape; the neck part being left open for filling and emptying. (This was simply twisted and held together with the hand, when the skin was to be immediately emptied; but it might be tied, when it was to be kept full, or carried to a distance.) All kinds of liquids, even wine and honey are kept in these skins.—This illustrates the parable of the new wine and old bottles, Luke v. 37, 38. The bottles were *skins*: and, as wine is a fermented liquor, the skin bottles, once used, would be so much impregnated with the wine that had been in them, that if new wine were put into them, it would cause it to ferment anew; and this would burst them. The original inmates of the hospital were now greatly reduced; a number having recovered, and a great many having died: but it was not allowed in any part to remain empty. Grand Cairo having surrendered to the British and Turkish forces on the 24th June, the sick of our own army were sent down the Nile; and they filled up all the vacancies. Cases of dysentery, and sore eyes, were so numerous, that a number of buildings were fitted up in Rosetta for their reception. Many died of the dysentery; but those afflicted with sore eyes were most numerous, and much to be pitied. Their torment was excessive: the pain in their eyes was as if they had been filled with burning sand; they had no respite from acute sufferings; and many lost their sight in spite of all the power of medicine. About the end of August, my own eyes became dreadfully inflamed in one night. The surgeon applied a very large blister in the morning, and by next day the inflammation was greatly subsided, but I did not get wholly free of it until I left Egypt, and was several days at sea on the way to Malta. The Egyptian *ophthalmia* was one of the most dreadful calamities that ever befel the British army.

The French that were in Cairo, amounting to 13,000, were embarked and sent to France in the month of August.

As my leg continued to mend, I felt grateful to God for his great mercy to me; but it was not long, until I had to accuse myself of having failed in duty, and come short of my promise; and this threw me into dejection of mind; which however wore gradually off. As I had much leisure time, I read more of my Bible than formerly; but the historical parts attracted my attention more than the doctrinal. Happening to read through the beginning of Exodus, I was struck when I found, that I had made use of the same words that Pharaoh used to Moses, chap. ix. ver. 28, and which he afterwards repeated, chap. x. ver 17. This made me fear, lest I should prove like Pharaoh; and in place of being softened by mercies, and bound by gratitude, become hardened by them and perish in the end. I then recollected, that I had heard Dr. Balfour preach, from Hebrews iii. 12, 13, I remembered the words, "*lest any of you be hardened through the deceitfulness of sin,*" and I turned to the passage and read it. It led me to ponder on the deceitful nature, and dangerous tendency of sin; which increased my fear that I might become hardened, and made my mind very uneasy. I would sometimes think on the instructions I had got, and the tasks I had learned at the Sabbath school; which I had now almost forgotten: I remembered some little of the xviith of John, for the learning of which, myself and others had received a penny. This led me to read it, and the liiid of Isaiah, which also I had learned; but I did not understand its import, although familiar with the words. I then turned over all the parallel passages, that I had read, in proof of doctrines in the school; and although I did not understand those that treated of the way of a sinner's acceptance with God, by faith in the righteousness and atonement of the great Redeemer, yet it helped to keep the words of Scripture relative to these doctrines on my memory, which was of use to me afterwards. But the doctrines of heaven, and hell, the resurrection, and eternal judgment, are more readily apprehended: and these made increasingly strong impressions on my mind.

I was now pretty certain that I was unfit for military service; and from Egypt, the land of bondage, I cast a longing eye to my native home, and wished myself there, that I might enjoy the benefits of a Sabbath, the instructions of religious teachers, and freedom from the society of the wicked. All my hopes now centered in this, and, had I despaired of it, I would have given myself over for lost.

After the French were embarked who had surrendered at Cairo, our troops which had been there, rejoined the army that was blockading Alexandria. Several regiments had lately come from England, so that it was now pretty strong. Alexandria was immediately besieged in form, and the operations pushed so vigorously, that the garrison was compelled to surrender on the 1st September, on condition of retaining their private property and being sent to France. Their number was about eleven thousand, of all descriptions. This event terminated hostilities in Egypt, and our troops prepared to leave it as soon as possible. Rosetta was occupied during the siege by a division of British, and Sepoys, natives of India, under the command of Sir David Baird, who had come from the East Indies to our assistance, with about seven thousand men. They had sailed up the Red sea, and marched through the desert, and arrived at Cairo shortly after it had surrendered. The Sepoys, when off duty, laid aside their uniforms, and walked about in the burning sun with nothing on the body but a pair of very short white drawers.

The dress of men and women of the common people of Egypt, consists of a blue cotton gown resembling a woman's shift; some have an upper and under garment. The men wear a sash or girdle round the middle; a turban and slippers; but no stockings. The women have no girdle round the middle; they wear vails; of which those that I saw were of coarse net-work, resembling the texture of a serjeant's sash, and shaped like the little bag nets used for catching trout in small rivers. The mouth of them is put under the chin and over the forehead, and is fastened behind: there are two holes opposite to the eyes, and the tapering end hangs down the breast. They appear to think, that modesty lies in concealing from public view the lower part of the face, whilst they are very negligent in other respects, which are more essential to that virtue. To Europeans the appearance of their faces, and particularly the part that is usually concealed, is no way interesting. Their complexion is dark ; their eyes, in general, are inflamed ; and their cheeks and chins are marked with the figures of half moons, stars, &c. in the way that our sailors mark themselves.

In some of the towns, girls, 14 years old, were seen going to the river for water, in a state of complete nudity; and males of all ages were seen mixed together in groupes, in the same state, without any sense of shame. They anoint their bodies with olive oil, which prevents the sun from blistering the skin. There are no stools or chairs for sitting upon in Egypt; their common way of sitting is upon the hams of their legs, in which posture they will remain for hours, apparently as much at their ease as a European upon a chair; they eat their meals in a reclining posture, but make no use of knives, forks or spoons; when they sup they literally " dip their hand in the dish,"* and feed themselves with their fingers in place of spoons. The above customs were practised in the time of Christ, and still exist through the east.

There are numbers of mosques, or Mahomedan churches, in the towns. They have, in general, a particular kind of spires, called minarets, some of which are very lofty ; they are in shape at the top like an onion, but have no weathercocks, nor clocks, nor bells ; of which latter, the Mahomedan religion prohibits the use. The minarets have all one or more balustrades round them, into which a man ascends at the end of every watch, and walks round, calling the people to prayers with as loud a voice as he possibly can. In Egypt it is commonly a blind man who performs this office.

The uninterrupted sunshine at Cairo, afforded the French the means of partly supplying the want of clocks and bells, by ascertaining exactly when it was twelve o'clock. They mounted one of the guns in the citadel upon a peculiar construction, and put some fine brass work at the breech, in which was a burning glass just over the touch hole ; by which the rays of the sun, the instant he reached the meridian, kindled the powder and fired the

* Mathew xxvi. 23.

gun. This is a proof that clouds and rain are seldom seen at Cairo; otherwise the firing of the gun could not have been depended on. When the French left the citadel, the Turks got possession of it; and some of them broke and stole the brass work of this gun, supposing the polished metal to be gold.

The heat of the country was very oppressive; and the army that went to Cairo suffered much from it during their march. The perspiration came through their clothes, and wetted their buff belts opposite the back, just as if they had been soaked in water.

About this time a very melancholy accident happened to some men of the 13th regiment of foot. Their regimental store house was in a building a few yards from the hospital; some of them were employed sorting cartridges in a room on the first floor, when one of them came in smoking tobacco, and thoughtlessly held his head over an open chest into which they were packing the cartridges; a spark fell from the pipe, and the powder exploded and gave a violent shock to the hospital and adjacent buildings; several men, and a serjeant's wife, were killed in the house, and I think nine or ten more were much bruised and dreadfully burned, and were brought into the hospital; their condition was more pitiful than that of those who were severely wounded, because so much of the skin of the face and body had been burned, that they had not sound skin left to lie upon; five or six of them lingered about a week in great agony, and died. I think, that twelve or sixteen were killed or severely injured by this accident. Some who were sitting in the bottom of an open window, with their legs over the wall, were blown down into the street, but were not much hurt.

Towards the end of September, my wound was nearly whole, but my leg was very much contracted. I was ordered to prepare to join my regiment at Alexandria to go home with it. But before taking a final leave of the hospitals, I would make a few further remarks upon the manner in which I saw my fellow creatures depart this life. And it must be confessed, that to all appearance many of them died *hardy;* they might groan through extremity of bodily pain, but did not exhibit any anguish of mind at the fear of death or judgment; but I could not discern any rational ground for this apparent want of anxiety about futurity. To make a merit of meeting death bravely, when it cannot be avoided, is but a poor reason for a rational, immortal, and accountable creature, to act upon. If man is a sinner, and must render an account to his Maker when he dies, surely to manifest no concern about the issue of death, is not to act the part worthy of a rational creature. To shut out all concern about eternity, in order to act the *hero* at the last, is liker the conduct of a blind madman than a true *hero;* for true courage in the hour of death can only be founded on the knowledge of our being happier hereafter; and this persuasion is only to be attained, by the reception of the good news of salvation by Jesus Christ, revealed in the Scriptures. Infidelity has said much against the superstition of the Bible; but while it does this, it gives an accountable creature nothing in the room of it upon which to found a reasonable hope for eternity. Infidels have often said that the fears of hell which make men afraid to die, are the produce of superstition. Were there none of those whom I saw die, who had freed themselves of the fears produced by the Bible account of a future state! It is likely that some of them had; for their previous habits and behaviour were as opposite to the Scriptures, as if they had never heard of such a book; and it was as little talked of, as if it had never existed. If infidelity be *true,* the death of its disciples ought to be more dignified and composed than that of any others: their future prospects ought to be the most certain, intelligent, and cheering to the immortal soul, when it is about to take its flight into the world of spirits and return to God who gave it. A dying infidel, if his system be *truth,* should be one that should rejoice in death, that he had freed himself from the fears produced by the Bible: he ought to be able to direct those around his dying bed to the truth that supports his mind, and show, at the same time, that he has a proper discernment of his own condition as an accountable creature, and suitable conceptions of the moral character of his Maker and Judge. But

of all that I ever saw die, I never heard any rejoicing in the
assertions of infidelity : I saw many die apparently *hardy ;*
but their deaths resembled more that of the beasts that
perish, than of accountable immortal creatures. I have
since seen Christians die, but the manner of their death
was very different: their conceptions of the majesty and
holy purity of God were exalted; their sense of the evil
of their own sins, and the moral responsibility of their
conduct, was deep; but with all this full in their view,
they had good hope through trusting in Christ ; and I never yet saw or heard of a dying Christian who regretted
that he had trusted too much to Christ, or thought too
highly of him; but the contrary. I have often heard them
regret deeply that they had thought too lowly of him,
and of what he had done to save sinners, and had trusted
too little to him, and depended too little on the promises
of the Bible ; and I have heard them pray earnestly for
forgiveness for this, as being the most heinous of all their
sins. Reader, if ever your mind has been stumbled by
the arguments of infidelity, try it by this test,—what
provision does it make for eternity, to a sinful and accountable creature; and you will find that in this most important
of all other concerns it makes no provision whatever:
it is revelation alone that either does or can make any
provision for a certain ground of hope for futurity. God
alone can tell how he will forgive sin : he has done this
in the Scriptures, and there alone. O be sure you examine what is revealed in them upon this subject, and
build your hope for eternity only upon what God has revealed to a sinner to trust in, that you may not die in
despair, nor be deluded by a false hope, and finally be
disappointed : and for this purpose, I earnestly entreat
your serious consideration of what is said towards the
conclusion of this narrative.

Before leaving the hospital, I feel bound in gratitude
to acknowledge the care and attention that was paid to
the sick and wounded : all things considered, every thing
was done for them that could be done, and much expense
was incurred for medicines, attendance, and accommodation, and every exertion made to procure suitable provisions. When I think upon it to this day, I feel grate-

ful for the care that was taken of the helpless, and those who were rendered unfit to serve their country any long-er : by this means many were preserved to their families and their friends, who otherwise would never have re-turned.

On the 29th September, I embarked in a Germ on the Nile, which dropped down the river, and lay near the en-trance, to be ready to pass the bar early in the morning, that being the most favourable time; for the wind rises at sun-rise, and blows from the sea up the river during the day, with a steady, and sometimes strong breeze, and dies away in the evening. Vessels going up the Nile carry a press of sail, and go at a great rate during the day, and stop at night : vessels going down the river lower their sails and yards, lay their broadside to the stream, and drift along with it. On the morning of the 30th, the wind and surf were so high, that it was unsafe to at-tempt passing the bar; so that we returned to Rosetta and lay at the quay three days, waiting for moderate weather. The Nile was still considerably above its banks : the extensive fields of rice, and corn, particularly on the east side, excited my admiration. The seed had been sown previously to the inundation, and had taken root and grown up with the rise of the water; which made it to have a compact and level surface, resembling that of a bowling green, for many miles. This crop would be ripe, by the time the inundation would fall within the banks of the river ; and another crop of wheat or barley, and one of clover or vegetables, would be produced be-fore the return of the inundation next year.—Water is raised by buffaloes and oxen from the river, into the ca-nals;* the beds of which are above the level of the

* I saw the buffaloes at this employment, when I sailed up the river, on the 24th June, when coming to Rosetta. The buffalo is much larger than the ox; his bones are uncommonly large, even in comparison to the size of his body, which is very lean; his strength must be much greater than that of the ox. When he walks, he carries his head like the camel, his nose being nearly as high as his horns, and is on the whole a very dull looking animal; but, notwithstanding, he is capable of being trained to this work, as well, if not better, than the ox ; for I saw them keeping a slow but steady pace at their work, with-out the immediate presence of a driver. The water is raised by a wheel, upon which buckets or earthen pitchers are fastened.

Since the publication of the first edition, I have seen the 5th vol. of country. It is let out into the fields during the growth of the other two crops; and when the last one is reaped, this labour is suspended. Then the heat of the sun soon dries the ground, and rends it into numerous and deep fissures; some of them are from ten to twenty feet deep. The army experienced considerable difficulty from this cause, on its march back from Cairo; particularly at night, when both men and horses were in danger of having their legs broke by falling into them.

While I lay at the quay, I was astonished at the great number of boats discharging cargoes of grain, which was piled in huge heaps in the open air, not far from the brink of the river;* a sight which reminded one of the words of Jacob, "I have heard that there is *corn* in Egypt." But, with all this plenty, it is a miserable place. The common people enjoy little of its abundance; their condition is the most wretched I ever saw or heard of among civilized nations. The houses of the peasantry are mere hovels, little if any thing better than the Kraals of the wild Hottentots.† The inhabitants of the land of

Dr. Clarke's Travels in Egypt; and as his knowledge is more extensive than mine, I take the liberty of inserting an extract, upon the produce and manner of cultivating the Delta. Speaking of the method of watering the ground, he says, "The land thus watered, produces three crops in each year; the first of clover, the second of corn, and the third of rice. The rice grounds are inundated, from the time of sowing nearly to harvest. The seed is commonly cast upon the water, a practice twice alluded to in sacred Scripture; *Balaam* prophesied of *Israel*, Numb. xxiv. 7, that "his seed should be in many waters." In the directions given for charity, by the son of *David*, it is written, Eccles. xi. 1. "Cast thy bread (*i. e.* bread corn) upon the waters: for thou shalt find it after many days." When the rice plants are about two feet high they are transplanted.—Vol. V. pp. 47. 48.

* The grain was measured by an Arab into baskets, which were carried to the heap by others, upon their shoulders. The measurer accompanied his work with a song indicative of the quantity he put into each basket. The owner stood upon the quay and received a bean or pea, from the carriers as they passed by him to the heap; and this was the method by which he kept an account of the quantity landed.

† I saw the exterior of some of these houses on the banks of the Nile, but never had an opportunity of seeing their interior. Sir R. Wilson says in vol. i, pp. 156, 157, "All language is insufficient to give a just idea of the misery of an Egyptian village; but those who have been in Ireland, may best suppose the degree, when an Irish hut

Egypt, which was the house of bondage to the children
of Israel, now suffer bondage in their own land, little, if
at all, inferior to that which their ancestors made the Is-
raelites suffer. The government has for a long time been
in the hands of Turks, or Mamelukes, who are always
foreigners, and who rule with rigour; and the inhabitants
never take any interest in the affairs of the government,
but are entirely passive to every change that takes place.
The country abounds with Arabs. The Copts, its original inhabitants, are the fewest in number; they profess
Christianity, and are the more liable, on that account, to
be oppressed by their Mahomedan masters. The pre-
diction is now fully verified, that Egypt, once the *first* of
nations, should become the *basest* of kingdoms : Ezek.
xxix. 15, 16. It is sunk so low in ignorance and wretchedness, that, if it were not for the many elegant and stu-
pendous remains of antiquity existing in the country,
the voice of history, strong as it is, could scarcely be
credited, that it was once the *first* of nations, and the
seat of the arts and sciences. It is a land of pestilence
and disease. " In Cairo, last year, forty thousand were
" supposed to be infected with the plague: and many of
" the French garrison died in that city, although the
" disease was treated in their hospitals with the greatest
" ability. In Upper Egypt sixty thousand perished dur-
" ing the same season,"* besides those who died of it in
other parts of the country. Among the British, the plague
was confined to the " hospital and troops stationary at
" Aboukir, where it broke out on the 12th April, and

is described as a palace, in comparison to an Arab's stye; for it can be
called by no other name. Each habitation is built of mud, even the
roof, and resembles in shape an oven : within is only one apartment,
generally of about ten feet square. The door does not admit of a
man's entering upright; but, as the bottom is dug out about two feet,
when in the room, an erect posture is possible. A mat; some large
vessels to hold water, which it is the constant occupation of the women
to fetch ; a pitcher made of fine porous clay, found best in Upper Egypt,
near Cunei, and in which the water is kept very cool ; a rice pan, and
coffee pot, are all the ornaments and utensils. Here, then, a whole
family eat and sleep without any consideration of decency or cleanliness; being, in regard to the latter, worse even than the beasts of the
field, which naturally respect their own tenements.
* Sir R. Wilson's History, vol. ii. p. 116.

" terminated on the 26th August. Three hundred and
" eighty, in the course of that time, were affected with
" it ; one hundred and seventy three died, and two hun-
" dred and seven recovered. The deaths chiefly fell on
" the orderlies, nurses, and other servants of the hospi-
" tals.* The plague raged again at Rosetta towards the
" fall of the year ; and numbers of the Sepoys died of
" it."† When a person is infected with the pestilence,
after the manner of Egypt, (Amos iv. 10,) the disease is indicated by two boils which are commonly in the
groin. In addition to the plague, " Leprosy of the
" worst species, and Elephantiasis, which swells the legs
" larger than a common bolster," and a number of other
diseases, are very general. " The number of blind is
" prodigious, nearly every fifth inhabitant has lost one
" eye, and many both. All the children have sore eyes,
" and Europeans do not escape better. The French at
" first had more than two thirds of their army affected
" with this malady ; and the English, during their short
" stay, had one hundred and sixty totally blind, and two
" hundred that lost one eye irrecoverably."‡ How many
more were affected with this dreadful malady among the
troops that remained in the country until the following year,
when it was wholly evacuated, I cannot tell ; but have reason to believe the number was considerable. Children must
suffer much during their infancy from the flies, because they
are unable to drive them from their eyes. I saw a woman going to the Nile for water, which she carried in a pitcher upon
her head : a naked child sat across her shoulders ; its little
hands were employed in holding by the head of its mother, to prevent itself from falling ; its eye-lashes were literally black with flies that were sucking at its eyes, as
they would do at sugar. They work themselves into the
inner coating of the eyelids of infants, which no doubt
causes some of them to lose their sight in their tender
years. In addition to flies, gnats and mosquitoes ; all
other kinds of vermin are incredibly numerous, and troublesome ; so much so, that, although there were nothing else

* Sir R. Wilson's History, pp. 115, 132.
† Ibid. p. 119.   ‡ Ibid. p. 121.

but them, they would make Egypt an uncomfortable country to live in. Although the French used all the freedom of conquerors, they were perfectly sick of it. When we landed, they supposed, that, after we had expelled them, we intended to retain possession of it ; and they sincerely pitied the lot of their supposed successors. They fought indeed bravely ; but it was not out of love to the country, but in subordination to military discipline, and for the honour of their arms ; but when compelled to surrender on condition of being sent home to France, they rejoiced in the event as a happy deliverance. And indeed it was no wonder ; for, in addition to the disagreeable nature of the climate, many of the military posts where they did duty, being in lonely sandy deserts, were so ill accommodated, and in all respects so uncomfortable, that to do service at them was fitter for being a punishment to men banished for their crimes, than for those who deserved well of their country.

Dr. Clarke sailed up the Nile on the 10th of August, 1801, when the river was beginning to overflow the country. The following extract corroborates all that I had heard related by my comrades, after they had returned from Cairo, and is so interesting, that it will gratify such readers as have not access to his work. After passing Rachmanie, he says, " Villages in an almost un
" interrupted succession, denoted a much greater popu
" lation than we had imagined this country to contain.
" Upon each side of the river, as far as the eye could
" reach, we saw fields of corn and rice, with such beau
" tiful groves, seeming to rise out of the watery plains, and
" to shade innumerable settlements in the *Delta*, amidst
" never-ending plantations of melons and all kinds of
" garden vegetables, that, from the abundance of its
" harvests, Egypt might be deemed the richest country in
" the world. Such is the picture exhibited to the
" native inhabitants, who are seasoned to withstand the
" disorders of the country, and can bear with indiffer
" ence the attacks of myriads of all sorts of noxious
" animals ; to whom mud and mosquitoes, or dust and
" vermin, are alike indifferent ; who, having never exper
" ienced one comfortable feeling in the midst of their

" highest enjoyments, nor a single antidote to sorrow
" in the depths of their wretchedness, vegetate, like
" the *bananas* and *sycamores* around them. But strangers,
" and especially the inhabitants of *Northern* countries,
" where wholesome air and cleanliness are among the ne-
" cessaries of life, must consider Eygpt as the most detestu-
" ble region upon earth.   Upon the retiring of the Nile,
" the country is one vast swamp. The atmosphere, is im-
" pregnated with every putrid and offensive exhalation,
" then stagnates, like the filthy pools over which it
" broods.   Then, too, the plague regularly begins; nor
" ceases, until the waters return again.*   Throughout
" the spring, intermitting fevers universally prevail.
" About the beginning of May, certain winds cover even
" the sands of the desert with the most disgusting ver-
" min.†   The latest descendants of Pharaoh are not yet
" delivered from the evils which fell upon the land, when
" it was smitten by the hands of Moses and Aaron ; the
" plague of frogs," the " plague of lice," the " plague of
" flies," the " murrain, boils and blains," prevail so, that
" the whole country is " corrupted," and " *the dust of*
" *the earth becomes lice, upon man and upon beast, through-*
" *out the land of Egypt.*" This application of the words

* " General *Le Grange* assured us, when on board the *Braakel,* that
" the ravages in the French army, caused by the plague, during the
" month of April, at one time, amounted to an hundred men in a sin-
" gle day.

† " Sir Sidney Smith informed the author (Dr. Clarke), that one
" night, preferring a bed upon the sand of the desert to a night's lodging
" in the village of Etko, as thinking he should be more secure from
" vermin, he found himself, in the morning, entirely covered by them.
" Lice and *scorpions* abound in all the sandy desert near Alexan-
" dria."   One of my comrades informed me, that when some of the
date trees were split at *Abukir,* for making the hospital, there were so
many lice in the hearts of them that they might have been gathered
in handfuls.   The frogs also were so abundant at some of the places
where the army halted between Rosetta and Cairo, that it was not
possible to get at the water in the river without treading upon them;
and at one place the camp ground was literally covered with black
beetles, to the no small annoyance of the soldiers in the tents, and the bed
frames and matts that we got new in the hospital in Rosetta in the end
of June, were so full of bugs, by the end of September, that they were
fit only to be burnt.

" of sacred Scripture affords a literal statement of existing
" evils, such an one as the statistics of the country do
" now warrant.   In its justification, an appeal may be
" made to the testimony of all those who have resided
" in the country during the very opposite seasons of its
" prosperity and privation ; during the inundation, and
" when the flood has retired, or before it takes place, in
" the beginning of the year.   At the period of the over-
" flow, persons who drink the water become subject to
" a disorder called " *prickly heat* :" this often terminates
" in those dreadful wounds alluded to in the sacred writ-
" ings, by the words " *boils and blains.*"   During the
" months of *June, July,* and *August,* many individuals
" are deprived of sight, owing to a disorder of the eyes
" peculiar to this country.   *Europeans,* having no other
" name for it, have called it *ophthalmia,* from the organs
" it affects.   There was hardly an individual who did not
" suffer, more or less, the consequences of this painful
" malady.   At this season, also, the dysentery begins to
" number its victims ; and although some be fortunate
" enough to escape the worst effects of this disorder, it
" proves fatal in many instances."*

Dr. Clarke's account of what he experienced at Cairo,
in the middle of August, is also interesting :—" The
" mercury in Fahrenheit's thermometer seemed at this
" time fixed.   It remained at 90° for several days, with-
" out the smallest perceptible change.   Almost every
" European suffered from inflammation of the eyes.
" Many were troubled with cutaneous disorders.   The
" prickly heat was very common.   This was attributed
" to drinking the muddy water of the Nile, the inhabi-
" tants having no other.   Their mode of purifying it, in
" a certain degree, is by rubbing the inside of the water-
" vessel with bruised almonds: this precipitates a portion
" of the mud, but it is never quite clear.   Many persons
" were afflicted with sores upon the skin, which were
" called " *boils of the Nile ;*" and dysenterical complaints
" were universal.   A singular species of *lizard* made its
" appearance in every chamber, having circular mem-

* Clarke's Travels, vol. v. pp. 56, 59.

L 3

" branes at the extremity of its feet, which gave it such
" tenacity, that it walked upon window-panes of glass,
" or upon the surfaces of pendent mirrors.* This re-
" volting sight was common to every apartment, whether
" in the houses of the rich or of the poor. At the
" same time, such a plague of flies covered all things
" with their swarms, that it was impossible to eat with-
" out hiring persons to stand by every table with feath-
" ers, or flappers, to drive them away. Liquor could
" not be poured into a glass ; the mode of drinking was
" by keeping the mouth of every bottle covered until
" the moment it was applied to the lips : and instantly
" covering it with the palm of the hand, when removing
" it to offer to any one else. The utmost attention to
" cleanliness, by a frequent change of every article of
" wearing apparel, could not repel the attacks of vermin
" which seemed to infest even the air of the place. A
" gentleman made his appearance before a party he had
" invited to dinner, with lice swarming upon his clothes.
" The only explanation he could give as to the cause,
" was, that he had sat for a short time in one of the boats
" upon the canal. Perhaps objection may be made to a
" statement even of facts, which refers to no pleasing
" theme ; but the author does not conceive it possible to
" give *Englishmen* a correct notion of the trials to which
" they will be exposed in visiting this country, without
" calling some things by their proper names."†

Before losing sight of the contest that was in Egypt, it
may not be amiss to glance at the unavoidable evils of
war. With the inhabitants we had no quarrel : our sole
object was to expel the French. But this could not be
done, without the peaceful inhabitants receiving, in many
cases, serious injury. The roads from town to town did
not suit the march of the army to and from Cairo ; the
troops generally took the direct road through the corn

---

* " A similar membrane terminates each foot of a common fly: be-
" neath which a vacuum takes place, and the animal maintains a
" footing upon ceilings, owing to the pressure of the external air upon
" this membrane.

† Clarke's Travels, vol. v. pp. 78. 80.

fields, and their encampments were sometimes in fields of corn, tobacco, poppies, sego, melons, indigo, &c. the produce of which, however valuable, was destroyed. Fuel was scarce; and the soldiers were necessitated to use whatever would burn. Stalks of tobacco, bean straw, and such like substances, were used to boil the kettles;* and in places where dry straw was difficult to be had, it was necessary to place guards at the entrances to the neighbouring villages or towns, to prevent the soldiers from unroofing the houses for wood to make fuel: and with all the attention of the officers, such was the necessity of the case, that injury could not always be prevented.

The discipline of the army was strict, and the general behaviour of the troops good; but many instances of petty depredations and pilfering took place, that were not known, and could not be prevented. Many instances occurred of inhabitants, particularly Arabs, who sold bread, fruit, eggs, &c. having their articles taken from them by " fellows of the baser sort," without any payment, and sometimes with abuse into the bargain. The Arabs when so used would throw dust upon their heads, and call upon God, and the Prophet, and the Sultan. But as this usage was not general, and as the army spent a considerable sum of good money among them,† they were not deterred from following it with whatever they had to sell, and I believe many of them made more money at that time, than ever they had an opportunity of doing before or since. On the afternoon of the 2d October, we again left Rosetta, and lay for the night near the mouth of the river. The wind was moderate next morning; we passed the bar safely: had a pleasant voyage

---

* When their rations happened to be salt pork, they used to put a piece of it under the kettle to burn with the straw.

† With the exception of gold, which was in the hands of a few, the coin circulating in Egypt was made of base metal, watered over with silver; and was of little or no intrinsic value. There were large pieces of this kind, some of them larger than a crown, which were of different values: but a small coin, called a para, about the breadth of a farthing, and no thicker than the scale of a fish, was the most common; of which 120, and in some places 160, were given for a Spanish dollar. The money expended by the army was gold and Spanish dollars.

128

across the bay of Aboukir and through lake Maadie;
passed through the cut in the banks of the canal of Alexandria into lake Mareotis* and landed not far from the
place where the battle of the 21st of March was fought,
of which I had thus another view, and which I never can
forget. I joined the regiment on the heights of Alexandria; we embarked next day at Aboukir, on board of
two frigates; sailed on the morning of the 7th October;
and lost sight of the celebrated land of Egypt by 12
o'clock. None regretted this. We indeed regretted our
countrymen and comrades, who had found a grave there;
but the country itself had no charms to make us regret
leaving it. All our thoughts were now fixed upon home;
and we rejoiced to think, that every day was bringing us
nearer it.

CHAPTER VII.

AFTER a pleasant passage, having light winds and fine
weather, we arrived at Malta on the 23d October. Here
our joy was wonderfully heightened by the news of peace.
The news had come from France, but they were credit-wor-
thy. The only cause of regret was, that such an important
and strongly fortified place as Malta, where we now lay,

* The inundation in this lake extended farther than the eye could
reach. The banks of the canal formed a road for communicating
with the interior of the country; a bridge of boats united the banks,
one of the boats being moveable, for the purpose of allowing vessels to
pass in and out of lake Mareotis. Before the army wholly left the
country, the boats forming the bridge were sunk in the cut, and served for a foundation upon which the banks were rebuilt. When the
British took Alexandria, in March 1807, a detachment was sent to take
Rosetta; but they were repulsed by those Turks who had accompanied
the army on its march to and from Cairo, and who had acquired a
considerable portion of British discipline. The rays of the sun had
by this time so far dried up the salt water in lake Mareotis as to render it passable; but the British again cut the banks of the canal, and
admitted the sea into it, to protect Alexandria from being attacked by
the Turks.

was to be given up ;—We did not leave Malta until the 26th November, at which delay the soldiers were vexed ; but the naval officers were no way anxious to get home, because they knew that the ship would be paid off, and they would then lose their situations. Our own officers were apprehensive that the regiment might be reduced, which would put them on half pay; but the men rejoiced in the prospect.* We had a tedious passage down the Mediterranean, and did not arrive at Gibraltar, until the 20th December. We left it on the 1st January, 1802, and arrived at the Cove of Cork on the 23d, having had rough weather all the way, which on two occasions increased to a tempest, and did the ship I was in considerable damage. We had to ride quarantine until the 9th February. My leg had stretched considerably during the passage, and I walked about the deck with the help of a stick. The regiment landed, and marched into Cork, on the 12th, the wounded and baggage being conveyed by water. And here I found that, although I could safely walk about with a stick on the level deck of a ship, my leg was not sufficiently strong, to travel the necessary distances on land. My wound here broke out again; and when the regiment left Cork for Kilkenny, although I rode upon the baggage, yet the travelling from the places where the baggage halted to my billet, which was sometimes more than a mile, was injurious to me. We came to Kilkenny on the 21st, and lay in it about six weeks. The regiment was inspected by the General and Surgeon of the district, and a great number ordered to be discharged, of which I was one.

My conduct in Kilkenny was not what it ought to have been ; not that I fell into open gross sin, but I did not improve my mercies as I ought, and was guilty of what I disallowed in my own conscience, and felt my weakness and inability to overcome the inward workings of corruption. I here bought Young's Night Thoughts, that by reading it, I might fortify my mind against temptation. I placed great confidence in the power of the

* The short duration of the peace, however, prevented the fulfilment of it.

poet's language; but it had not the effect I wished and expected. I was one evening at the Methodist chapel; but I did not pay that attention to the Sabbath which I might have done. The regiment left Kilkenny, and marched for Belfast; and when we came to Dublin, the discharged men that were recommended to the benefit of Chelsea Hospital, embarked for Liverpool, from which we proceeded to London; where I was examined and admitted an out-pensioner of Chelsea Hospital, on the 27th May, 1802. I left London on the 29th, and took a passage in one of the Carron Company's brigs; landed at Queensferry on the 12th of June, and arrived in Glasgow next day, happy to find myself restored to my friends.— My wound was still open; I might have gone into York hospital in London, and been cured, previously to being discharged; and had I been wise, I should have done this: but I was so anxious to be home, that I did not do it, for fear it might delay me some time.

My military life being now terminated, I desire to bless God, with a grateful heart, for his goodness and care over me while in the army, in a particular not before referred to. For during the six years that I was a soldier, I was never confined for any fault. My conduct was, in general, good, in a military point of view; but there were times that I was guilty of faults, for which I might have been punished, and which I have reason to thank God for escaping. And what is a little singular, I was never concerned in any court martial case, nor so much as a witness against any man: on the whole, I passed comparatively easy and quietly through the army, and without doubt, the remaining restraints of early religious instruction was one particular mean of preserving me from many evils and dangers; and in this respect proved an invaluable blessing to me, while I was a soldier. I mention this particular to show what good early religious instruction may do, although it may not have the effect of converting the soul.

I had now attained my wishes, by being safely settled at home. God had given me the desire of my heart. If I did not now find ability to keep the commandments of God, in the way that I proposed to myself, and upon which I founded my hope of meriting and enjoying his favour, I could not expect to find any situation more favourable. I called to mind all the promises I had made, and reflected on all the deliverances God had graciously given me. and the gratitude that was due to him for them. Circumstances led me to attend Mr. Ewing's ministry at the Tabernacle; but, although I attended divine ordinances, and read religious books, I was not a whit the better. I had also considerable opportunity of being alone; but where I thought I would be strongest, there I found I was weakest; and, when removed from outward temptation, inward corruption increased, and baffled my utmost efforts. The more I strove to keep my own heart and life from sin, the more sin triumphed over me. I found, in my experience, that I was a slave to sin; for what I set myself to overcome, overcame me. At the same time, the spirituality of God's law increasingly opened on my mind; I daily saw more of the extent of the work I had assigned to myself to perform, in order to obtain the favour of God; and found that my practice, in place of getting nearer, was getting farther from it. When I looked back on the mercies I had received, and the promises and resolutions I had made, I saw that I had all along been mocking God, having never fulfilled any of them. This broke my peace of mind; I became more subject to the terrors of the law than I had ever been; my conscience accused me of the blackest ingratitude; I had no refuge to fly to; my sins became too heavy for me; the justice of God stared me in the face; and now I saw that I was a condemned criminal. I gave over all hope of obtaining the favour of God by my own doings; I resolved to mock him with no more promises of amendment of life; I confessed that hell was what I deserved; that the law which condemned me was just: and, when I did this, the importance of being delivered from such a dreadful situation was increasingly impressed upon my mind: but how to obtain that deliverance I could not tell. I saw by the Scriptures, that "unless a man be born again, he cannot enter into the kingdom of God," and that no unholy being shall enter heaven. I prayed earnestly for the new heart and the right spirit, but did not correctly understand in what this change consisted. I passed a considerable time subject to sharp conflicts in my mind, during which, the stings of conscience and the terrors of the law were beyond description : but all was kept within my own breast, without being discerned by any one. My leg continued badly until the beginning of 1803, when I confined myself to bed for some weeks, and had the pleasure once more of seeing it heal. I felt thankful to God for this new mercy ; but it added fresh torment to my mind, for it furnished my conscience with new matter of accusation. In perusing Boston's " Fourfold State," I was startled at reading how the branches are taken out of the natural stock. I saw my own case pretty fully described ; but as I did not understand what it was to be " apprehended of Christ," and united to the vine, it only increased my uneasiness. I also heard a man in conversation in my company declare, that, before a sinner can be brought to God, the same power behoved to be exerted that converted the apostle Paul. I did not assent to what he said, because I did not believe it ; but I marked the saying. I became increasingly uneasy ; I had no peace in my mind ; eternity was before me ; I was without hope, and knew not how to obtain it. " *What*," said I " *shall become of me!*" I was agitated almost to despair ; all that prevented me from falling into it was the consideration that I was yet in life, and that God had not forbidden me to cry for mercy : and for mercy I did cry, if peradventure I might find it.

My leg now threatened to break out again. This alarmed me more, and it prevented me from going, as I had done, to the Tabernacle. The forenoon of the second Sabbath after Albion-street chapel was opened, I passed solitary at home ; but I was in a most painful state of mind, of which the agitations cannot be described. My convictions of sin were so sharp as to drive me into a state, which, if it was not absolute despair, could hardly be distinguished from it. I could not bear my own presence, and became afraid to be alone. " *What shall become of me!*" was the unremitting thought of my agitated soul. It at length drove me to my knees ; where, with tears, I confessed my sins to God without reserve or palliation ; fully acknowledged the righteousness and justice of his law; disclaimed all merit of my own; confessed that I never had any, nor any ability to obtain it; that I was totally unable to do any thing to procure his favour, or to recompense him for it, should he bestow it; and that if I was saved from endless woe, it would be, because he would have mercy on me, out of his own sovereign pleasure, and not on account of any merit of mine. I cast myself upon his pure mercy, and confessed that if there was not pure mercy for sinners, I could have no hope.—When I arose from my knees, it was near the time of the afternoon's service. I felt quite uneasy at home. I thought I would venture as far as to Albion street chapel, because it was at no great distance, and because I had heard my father speaking favourably of you as a preacher. I was the more disposed too to go there, because I knew you were in connexion with Mr. Ewing, of whom I had formed a favourable opinion. When I got to the chapel, I was all attention. When you prayed, I endeavoured to pray also. But nothing particularly affected me, until you gave out your text, 1 Cor. ii. 2. "For I determined not to know any thing among you, save Jesus Christ and him crucified."—I was struck with the text, and became anxiously attentive, to see if I could catch any thing from the discourse which was to follow, that could give ease to my troubled mind. You had preached from it the preceding sabbath, and having recapitulated what you had gone over, you proceeded to the remainder of the subject; the tenor of which was, *the nature of the work that Christ had accomplished in the room of sinners, for their salvation.* As you proceeded, I thought I began to discern something I had not seen before. But when you proved from the Scriptures, that the work which Christ had finished on mount Calvary, was of itself sufficient to save sinners, and that God had accepted his work as satisfactory to him; that, therefore, the work of Christ being perfect, nothing could be added to it; that it was impious to attempt to add any thing to it, and that sinners ought to rest satisfied with that which God had declared was satisfactory to him, seeing he knew best what was necessary to satisfy his justice, and to secure his own honour in pardoning sin-

M

ners; that no good works were required of the sinner by
God, *as the ground of his acceptance with him*, either in
whole or in part, but that it was the merit of the work
of Christ alone, that justified sinners in the sight of a holy
God, and that all the praise of their salvation belonged
to Christ, and to the grace of God in him; and that sinners should believe this doctrine as good news, and put
their trust in it for the salvation they needed.—You I
think spoke also of the effect which the faith of this doctrine had on all them that believed it, in leading them to
love God, and to keep his commandments. I was greatly
enlightened by the whole discourse; but my mind particularly catched the words, that the work of Christ was of
itself perfect; that nothing could be taken from it, or added
to it; and that it was impious to attempt to add any thing to
it. This doctrine appeared new to me. I thought I had
never heard it before. I left the chapel when the service
was over, repeating to myself the words, " *The work of
Christ is perfect, sufficient of itself to save a sinner ;*" and, as
I repeated it, I said, " This is good news if it be true."
Another thought now started into my mind :—If it be true
that nothing can be added to it, and that it is impious to
attempt it, how guilty have I been!'—My whole train of
repentances, promises, resolutions, and attempted reformations, has not only been sinful in the sight of God, on account of their failures, but have been impious acts of rebellion ; not on account of my endeavouring to forsake sin, and
to cultivate holiness, but on account of the motive that produced them, which was a desire to work out a righteousness
of my own, to the rejecting of the righteousness of Christ;
placing my works on a level with his, nay above his; seeking to merit God's favour by my own doings ; and when
doubting of their complete sufficiency, having recourse to
the merits of Christ, merely to make up the deficiency of
mine; and even this, not from voluntary choice, but from a
feeling of necessity. This was a new source of guilt to my
conscience, which had never burdened it before. I began
to apprehend I had been guilty of the sin of unbelief, so
often spoken of in the Scriptures, and so strongly condemned. But while my conscience accused me of this, a gleam
of hope dawned on my soul, by ruminating on the suffi-

l

ciency of the work of Christ; and the more I pondered on the subject, my hope increased, and the more my hope increased, the stronger my sense of the sin of unbelief grew. These two things kept pace with one another: and while hope cheered my heart, this new sense of guilt made me humble. I did not think less of the guilt of my other sins; but this sin seemed to outweigh them all, so that I became increasingly vile in my own sight.

I read the Scriptures, with prayer to God for light and direction, that I might truly judge the doctrine I had been hearing, and not be led astray by that which was not his own truth. I compared scripture with scripture; and I now found the very great benefit of being acquainted with the letter of the Bible, and of having much of it on my memory. My meditations were greatly assisted by what was stored in it; for when employed at my work, I often recollected passages, and compared them together. All the drift of my thoughts, was to find if there was evidence of the sufficiency of the work of Christ, for a sinner's salvation; and in many of these passages I found such evidence: they appeared to me in a new light; and the sense was so obvious, that I wondered how I had not seen it before This new discernment gradually increased; and, as my wound did not break out, I continued to attend Mr. Ewing's ministry, and was growing in knowledge by means of his sermons. One of them was particularly blessed to me. It was an evening sermon from Matth. iii. 17. " And lo, a voice from heaven, which said, This is my beloved Son, in whom I am well pleased." The moment the text was read, I catched the words, "*in whom I am well pleased.*" I saw them, as containing a proof of God's satisfaction in the work of his Son on the behalf of sinners; I followed the preacher through the discourse, and was at no loss to comprehend his meaning; the doctrine was plain and evident to me. I had still, however, some perplexity in my mind, about the nature of the good works to be performed after believing. But this was removed by a sermon from Mr. Greig* from Heb. iii. 14. " For we are made partakers

* Then assistant to Mr. Ewing; now minister of the congregation in Crown Court, London.

of Christ, if we hold the beginning of our confidence
stedfast unto the end." My mind now became decided; I
saw that if a sinner had Christ, he had all. I was sweet-
ly constrained to give myself wholly up to him; to be
content to be saved by his merits, to the entire and eternal exclusion of my own; to place my hope of acceptance with God, both now and hereafter, solely upon *his*
perfect righteousness, and complete atonement; and to
commit my polluted soul to the gracious influence of his
Spirit, that he might so apply the blood of Christ, as to
" purge it from dead works, to serve the living God." I
now saw that deliverance from sin itself, was a part of
the salvation of Christ: and I was led to trust in him for
sanctification, as well as for righteousness and redemption.
I now understood clearly what had puzzled me, when I read
the book on Contentment, in Athlone. I was no longer
at a loss to understand what it was to be willing to *do* all
things for Christ, and to be willing to *deny* all things for
Christ. I saw that Christ is his people's strength; that
the power which enables them to perform duty, to resist
temptation, and to overcome their spiritual enemies, is
wholly derived from him; that therefore when they con-
quer their enemies, and bring forth the fruits of righteousness, the glory of the conquest belongs to him through
whose strength they have been performed. I therefore
esteem it my high privilege as well as duty, to " count all
things but loss for the excellency of the knowledge of
Christ Jesus my Lord; for whom" I trust I have, in a
measure, been made willing to " suffer the loss of all
things, and to count them but dung, that I may win
Christ, and be found in him, not having mine own righteousness which is of the law, but that which is through the
faith of Christ, the righteousness which is of God by faith."
Phil. iii. 9, 10.

My next concern was, about the question,—What is
the proper form of church government?—I had been made
a little acquainted with the claims of Episcopacy, and
they perplexed me a good deal. Upon the general question, my stock of information was small. This much I
knew, that all parties referred a good deal to the Acts of
the Apostles, for proofs of their respective opinions; and,

as Mr. Ewing had commenced a course of lectures upon that book, I hoped to obtain such information, as should enable me to come to a determination in my own mind. I continued to hear him with a good deal of interest, until he had gone through the fifteenth chapter. I then embraced his opinions on that subject; and, feeling the want of Christian fellowship, I determined to make present conviction the rule of present duty; and seeing that it was the will of Christ that his people should be united together in fellowship, I resolved to apply to Mr. Ewing, for admission to the church under his care. Being at a loss from my ignorance of the mode of application, and entire want of acquaintance with any of the members of his church, I wrote him a letter. This introduced me to a conversation, with which he was satisfied, and my case was to be mentioned to the church at their next meeting. I had no sooner returned home, however, than the words of Jesus, John iv. 36. " And he that reapeth receiveth wages, and gathereth fruit unto life eternal; that both he that soweth and he that reapeth may rejoice together," occurred to my mind. This led me to remember you, my dear Sir, through whom I had received the knowledge of the truth, and to consider whether there was not a propriety, if not a duty, rather to apply to the church under your care, for admission, than to Mr. Ewing's. I determined to consider this point, and wrote to Mr. Ewing, requesting him to delay mentioning my case to his church, as something had occurred to my mind, which it appeared to be my duty previously to consider, but as soon as I should come to a determination I should let him know. I then attended your preaching, to see whether it would be as beneficial to me as Mr. Ewing's. You were then lecturing in the forenoons through the 1st Epistle of John. As I was but a babe in Christ, doctrinal subjects were what I stood most in need of. I found myself edified by your discourses, and I felt an increasing attachment to you as my spiritual father; and, as we were of one mind on matters of church order, it appeared clearly to be my duty to seek for admission into your church. Every tie of spiritual affection seemed to require it. You had, through the blessing of the great Head of the church, sowed to

me the words of eternal life : I through his blessing had
reaped them ; and, as there was no obstacle betwixt us,
love said it was most proper, that he that sowed and he
that reaped should rejoice together ; for where should a
convert to the truth seek to be, but under the care of the
instrument that converted him ? There must be a pecu-
liarity of affection, betwixt a spiritual father and his children, beyond that of others placed under his care and instruction. This peculiar affection had now begun to ope-
rate in my mind ; for at first I had been so much taken
up with the discovery of the truth itself, that I had paid
little attention to the instruments who preached it, but I
now found leisure to give them a place, in their various
degrees, in my affections, without losing any regard for
the truth, or for its great Author and object, Jesus Christ,
the Chief Shepherd of the sheep. In order therefore
to strengthen your hands in the work of an under shepherd, as well as for my own benefit, I drew up a sum-
mary narrative of my life and experience, and of the way
in which it had pleased the Lord to lead me to a knowledge of his precious truth, and sent it to Mr. Ewing,
with the reasons why I thought it my duty to apply for
admission to your church. These reasons Mr. Ewing
approved of ; he gave you that narrative to introduce
me to you; and I was soon favoured with being admitted
under your pastoral care. The narrative is now greatly
enlarged; but before bringing it to a close I wish to make
a few general remarks.

I would begin with stating, that the belief of that doctrine which gave peace to my troubled conscience, gave
also a degree of stability to my conduct, such as I had
never before been able, with my utmost efforts, to attain.
Not but that I have still to lament, that sin dwells in me ;
but, by the grace of God, it does not reign over me, as
formerly; and the less I think of myself, and the lower
I estimate my own strength, and the more I trust to the
gracious promise of imparted strength, from the compas-
sionate and all powerful Redeemer, the stronger I am.
Whilst I rejoice in the possession of the new man, I have
still to mourn the existence of the old ; I find in my experience increasing evidence of the deceitfulness and

desperate wickedness of the heart, and see increasing
reason to be vile in my own eyes, and to pray continually
" God be merciful to me a sinner," but I trust in his
grace, that he will " fulfil in me all the good pleasure of
his goodness, and the work of faith with power," and
" preserve me by his power, through faith unto salvation,"
enabling me to maintain the war of the spirit against the
flesh, until I get a complete and eternal victory.

And here I must express my gratitude to God, for the
benefit of Christian fellowship, and of pastoral care and
instructions. It is now about sixteen years since I first
heard you preach, and became a member of the church
under your ministry. We have had our trials, to exercise our forbearance and patience ; but we have also had
our comforts. I still love the brethren, and while I say,
" Grace be to all them who love our Lord Jesus Christ
in sincerity," I wish for no other fellowship ; and while I
love all who preach Christ crucified, as the only ground
of a sinner's acceptance with a holy God, yet I desire no
other teacher than he who first turned my wandering
feet into the way that leadeth to life   Your instructions
and warnings have, I trust, enabled me to keep in that
way with my face Zionward.   May the Lord grant, that
we may continue to walk together, and be, in our respective stations, comforts to each other on the road,
until we arrive at the heavenly Jerusalem ;—and there
may I be one of those, who shall be to you, " a
crown of joy and rejoicing in the presence of the Lord !"
There may we rejoice together, in the rich mercy of the
great Redeemer, and give him all the praise, for converting and preserving grace, both in the convert and in him
who was the instrument of his conversion ; and may you
have many more in whom to rejoice, besides the subject
of this narrative ! I thank God for the success with which
he has been pleased to bless your labours. There are
not a few, who now sit under your ministry, who have
received the knowledge of the truth by means of your
preaching ; and others, I believe, have joined the church
above. May the Lord grant you increasing success in
turning sinners to God, and in edifying saints ; may he
bless the labours of all his servants and people ; and may

his own word have free course and be glorified, by the
overturning of the kingdom of sin and of Satan in the
world; and may the " kingdoms of this world soon become the kingdoms of our Lord and of his Christ." Amen.

I remain, Dear Pastor,

Your Affectionate Son

In the Faith of the Gospel,

G. B.

GLASGOW, January, 1819.

To the
Rev. RALPH WARDLAW.

POSTSCRIPT.

HAVING now finished my narrative, may I take the liberty of adding a few reflections, with a view to direct the
minds of those who may read it, to the lessons I should
wish them to learn from it.

There are two things which are conspicuous in it; the
first is, a sinner's *weakness;* the second is, a sinner's
blindness.—It shows how long and how often I attempted
to cleanse my own heart. I made the effort under all the
variety of circumstances I have mentioned, but all in
vain. I acted under all the motives I could collect from
a sense of the glory, goodness, justice, and general mercy of God, as displayed in the works of creation and
providence; and also from what I had learned from the
Bible of the requirements of the moral law, which was
often like a fire in my conscience; and from a fear of
hell and eternal judgment, and a desire of heaven and
eternal life; and from a sense of mercy to myself in
being so often protected when in imminent danger, delivered out of trouble, and brought back from the very
jaws of death in answer to my prayers for mercy :—yet
all these put together were insufficient to keep me from
breaking the commandments of God, and being guilty
of what I condemned in my own conscience. And thus

it will be with every sinner, that sets himself to perform the same task. I do not refer to *my* experience, as an exclusive proof of this; but I refer to it as an instance of the truth of God's word, which declares that sinners are "*without strength.*" Rom. v. 6. Let any sinner undertake the same task, and I can assure him from the word of God, that he will come no better speed. He may attempt it again and again; but every new attempt will only show his weakness and blindness; and, as he proceeds, he will find that he was not aware of the ten thousandth part of the extent and difficulty of the task. If he persevere in it, he will find it necessary, after endeavouring to reform his outward conduct, to look *within,* and there he will discover work he was not at first aware of. He will find it absolutely indispensable to watch over his *heart* if he means to reform external conduct: for it is the heart that first yields to temptation. And, let his resolutions be ever so strong, and his intentions ever so sincere, he will find that the slightest temptations are sufficient to overcome him. Nor will he be in danger from outward temptations only; for although he were in the retirement of a hermit, and totally secluded from the world, he would find temptations to sin rising spontaneously out of *that very heart* which had formed the resolution not to commit it; he would find himself led like a captive to the commission of it, and that in the face of the clear light of duty, and in spite of the strongest remonstrances of conscience; thus giving him the most convincing evidence, if he had eyes to see it, that " the heart is deceitful above all things, and desperately wicked;" (Jer. xvii. 9.) that " he that committeth sin is the servant (or slave) of sin ;" (John viii. 34.) and that " he that trusteth in his own heart is a fool." (Prov. xxviii. 26.) So long, however, as a sinner has any confidence in his own strength, he will not renounce it, in order to depend upon strength to be imparted from another. So long as he fancies any merit in his own works, he will trust to them to procure his Maker's favour. But in this he only shows his blindness. O that I could convince any into whose hands this narrative may fall, to renounce, as entirely hopeless, all such efforts; and also as

entirely worthless, all such attempted reformations; and
to flee to the all-mighty and all-meritorious Redeemer!
You need his perfect righteousness to justify you, and his
blood to atone for your sins; you need the gracious in-
fluences of his Spirit to purify your hearts, and to give
you strength to walk in the ways of God : for the motive
to obedience that alone can enable you to walk with sted-
fastness and consistency, arises out of the belief of the
love of Christ, in giving himself a ransom for the guilty.
The belief of this will inspire you with love to him in return ; and this, and this alone, will set your souls at liberty from the slavery of sin.   It is to those who believe
the love that he manifested in freely giving himself a sacrifice for them, that he imparts strength to resist temptation; and he warns all his disciples that " without him
they can do nothing."   He has promised his grace as
sufficient for them that trust in him in the most trying situations, and to perfect his strength in their weakness :—
nor is this an empty promise ; for he, to whom it was
more immediately addressed, declared that " he could
do all things through Christ who strengthened him ;" and
the way in which he obtained the power was, by being
conscious of his own weakness, and trusting entirely to
the promised strength of the Saviour ; " for," says he,
" when I am weak then am I strong." 2 Cor. xii. 7—10.
with Phil. iv. 13.—Go you and do as he did ; and you
will find that Christ will be the same to you that he was to
him, for the Saviour is unchangeable; " the same yesterday, and to-day, and for ever." Heb. xiii. 8.

I have been minute in detailing the exercises of my
mind, much more so than some may think there is any
need for.   I have been induced to this in order to show
how long and how strenuously a sinner may go on in that
course, although his efforts are constantly failing ; and
fail they must, so long as his hopes terminate on himself,
and so long as he refuses to put his entire confidence in
the Saviour.   He may give over the task in despair, and
sink into carelessness and indifference ; but if, whilst he
finds his hopes of himself fruitless, he is still convinced
of the importance and necessity of the salvation of his
soul, and feels that he is one ready to perish; then the

news of a Saviour will be glad tidings to him indeed ; and with the death of his legal hopes a life of evangelical obedience will commence.—I have been induced to be minute, from a desire to shew to others the folly of continuing to labour in the fire, as I did, for very vanity; and that they may see the necessity of fleeing directly to the Saviour. If you are saved at all you *must* do this at the last ; and why not to-day as well as to-morrow, or any future period? Jesus says " To-day if ye will hear my voice, harden not your hearts :" he says, " Come unto me, all ye that labour and are heavy laden, and I will give you rest." And why will ye not hear his voice, and accept of his invitation to-day ? If you reject him to-day, you may not live till to-morrow. All the offers of the gospel are *present offers* ; there is no promise respecting to morrow. Jesus is as able to day as to-morrow. He offers himself to-day. His salvation is a present salvation. " Behold, now is the accepted time; behold, now is the day of salvation."

If any read this narrative, who are putting off the concerns of their immortal souls to a death-bed, and are deluding themselves with the notion, that the distress of a sick-bed and the fear of death will break the power of sin in their hearts, and that they will then repent and believe; while you think this, you shew that you do not know what repentance and faith are ; for, did you know what they are, you would already have repented and believed. You cannot know them until you are in actual possession of them. Your conduct is, therefore, ignorant and presumptuous. Faith and repentance are present duties ; and if you will not repent of your sins *now*, and believe in the Lord Jesus Christ for salvation, what security have you that you will do so hereafter ? you may be brought to a sick-bed : and there, the approach of death, and the fear of hell, and remorse of conscience, arising out of convictions of sin, may greatly alarm you; but this will not change your heart, nor save your soul. Such a state of mind is neither repentance nor conversion. How often was I in danger, and imagined I repented ; and, when I was at the point of death, I thought I had repented in truth. But my conduct after I had recovered showed that I had deceived myself; and had I died in the state I then was in, I must have perished. When you are laid on a sick-bed, you may find that you have no hope of heaven if you die at present; you may wish to recover, that you may change your conduct; you may cry to God to spare you; but he may not hear you; and when you see that death is actually approaching, you may be driven to despair, and die without hope: or, in order to calm a troubled conscience, you may persuade yourselves that you have repented, and that, as you are not allowed to live, God will accept of the sincerity of your repentance; and you may thus " go down to the grave with a lie in your right hand." But if you despise the offer of a Saviour now, and put off these things to a death-bed, which many never see, but are called suddenly out of the world, the probability is, that when you are actually laid upon it, however old you may be, and however evident the approach of your latter end may be to all who see you, you will not think you are going to die *yet*, but will still indulge the hope of longer life;—until death lays his cold hand on your heart, and closes your eyes for ever on a present world.

Should this narrative fall into the hands of any who are in the army, I would earnestly entreat them to lay the contents of it seriously to heart, and to beware of the delusive idea that it is not needful to be religious in the army. Although you are soldiers, you are still surely under the government of your Creator. Your being in the army will not excuse the sins you commit in it. There is no article of war that commands you to swear, or to get drunk, or to be guilty of uncleanness, or any other sin. There is no order that prohibits you from repenting of your sins, and believing on the Lord Jesus Christ for the salvation of your invaluable souls, and living a life of faith upon the Son of God; so that you are without excuse. Your being in the army does not give you a greater security of long life to be an excuse for delay. On the contrary, *you*, above all men, ought to secure the salvation of your immortal souls. And blessed be God, that salvation is offered as freely to you as to others. Jesus, the King of kings, offers you his free and unmerited favour, in the same way that he does to others; and makes you as welcome. Your souls are as precious to him, as those of any of the human race: so that you are without excuse. Beware of another delusion;—that the army is a place in which it is impossible to live a godly life. This is not true. However hard it is, yet it *is* possible, and has been done. If indeed you attempt to live a godly life in your own strength, as I did, you will fail ; but remember, so would you in any situation in which you could be placed. But if you believe in the Lord Jesus, and take him for "righteousness and *strength*," he will fulfil to you his promise, that " as your day is, so shall your strength be." Remember that the way that leadeth to eternal life is a narrow way to all ; and that the same grace which enables others to travel that narrow way is sufficient to enable you to travel it also ; and that the same power which brings others safely through, is able to carry you also in safety to the end of the journey. Remember that it is the power of God and not of man that enables *any* to persevere unto the end; and will you say that it is not in the power of the Almighty to enable a soldier to serve him in the army, and to lead a Christian life in it ? The idea is blasphemous; it is a delusion of Satan; and it is an unjust charge upon the army, bad as it is, and one of the greatest obstacles, if not the very greatest, to its moral improvement ; for it goes to prevent the very attempt at improvement, as utterly hopeless, and consequently to leave the individuals who compose it to be confirmed in all their evil habits. If any soldier read this, let me beseech him to lay seriously to heart the immense value of his soul, and to believe in the grace and power of a Redeemer ; and, although there should not be one godly person in his regiment, let him not be afraid to believe in Jesus, and to regulate his conduct by his word. Do not be afraid of the mocking of your comrades : it is indeed not easy to bear ; but if you really trust in Christ, he will enable you to live down their reproaches by a consistent and steady course of life. *Their* reproaches are not to be put in comparison with *his* smiles: and if the King of kings smiles upon you, what need you care who frowns ? It will become you rather to pity, than to be offended at them. Seek, by constant prayer, for that prudence and wisdom which will enable you so to act as to put to silence their foolish scoffings; and, if you persevere, you will extort from them so much commendation as will repay you for all the reproaches you have borne, or may still be subject to. But let your faith be constant and your practice persevering. Do not take up religion by fits and starts. Those who do so shew that they have not yet understood what it is. Unless your repentance be that of the Bible, and your faith in Jesus genuine, arising from a scriptural understanding of your own character as a guilty and helpless sinner in the sight of God, and a scriptural discernment of the rich grace and almighty power of Christ, you will not be able to stand : for the army is not a place for hypocrites, formalists, and self-righteous professors, to prosper in. The professions of such will generally vanish like smoke. The genuine believer in Jesus alone is able to abide the trial ; and he stands, because he is upheld by the power of God through faith unto salvation. Therefore, let no soldier neglect his salvation, through fear that the temptations of the army will be too much for him. Great as they are, if he trusts in Christ, he shall be made "more than a conqueror through him that loved him ;" and the more he can get his comrades to attend to the same things, the temptations will diminish. And the more the religion of Jesus prevails in the army, and the greater the number of genuine disciples are in it, the greater improvement will be made in its character, efficiency, and comfort.

I rejoice that the army is beginning to be more attended to of late, in a religious point of view. I rejoice to see Bible Societies in operation for the benefit of the army and navy ; and wish them an increasing measure of success. The attention of the religious world has not yet been sufficiently drawn to the importance of the object. I hope that the stimulus that has been put in motion will continue to increase, and that a succession of prudent measures will be adopted for the promotion of the fear of God in the army and navy. The same means that are effectual for the attainment of this great object amongst the other classes of mankind will be effectual here. And what a blessing would it be to the army and navy, were the fear of God their prevailing character! How would it promote subordination, peace, sobriety, and chastity, and, in so doing, prevent the frequency and necessity of punishments and rigorous regulations, and the prevalence of those diseases which break the constitutions of such numbers, renders them non-effectives, and sends so many of them to an early grave!—And how much benefit would instantly accrue to society, in the reduction of the contamination of profanity, intemperance, and lewdness! How many female characters would be preserved, and the consequent grief of parents prevented! How much of the evil of prostitution would it reduce, which is so dangerous to youth in sea-port towns, and large cities! If my feeble voice could be heard, I would add it to that of those who have already appeared as advocates of this cause, in supplicating British Christians to prosecute this object with prudent but vigorous perseverance. I rejoice to see a floating chapel provided upon the Thames for the instruction of seamen. This, I hope, will be followed by similar measures wherever they are necessary. The wisdom that devised this, is competent to devise all that is wanting for the prosecution of this great cause, throughout the army and navy. And the same motives are sufficient to carry those embarked in it forward with zeal until the fear of God finally triumph. And its triumph in the army and navy will remove one of the obstacles to its prevalence in the world. And who knows but that genuine piety may not only prevail but even shine most conspicuously in the army and navy, and that the *last* may become *first*.

G. B.

FINIS.